the greatest catch

the greatest catch

a life in teaching

penny kittle

FOREWORD BY TOM ROMANO
AFTERWORD BY CHRIS CRUTCHER

HEINEMANN • PORTSMOUTH, NH

HEINEMANN
A division of Reed Elsevier Inc.
361 Hanover Street
Portsmouth, NH 03801–3912
www.heinemann.com

Offices and agents throughout the world

The author and publisher wish to thank those who have generously given permission to reprint borrowed material:

"Confessions" by Penny Kittle from *Voices in the Middle* (September, 2004). Copyright © 2004 by the National Council of Teachers of English. Reprinted with permission.

Library of Congress Cataloging-in-Publication Data
Kittle, Penny.
The greatest catch : a life in teaching / Penny Kittle; foreword by Tom Romano; afterword by Chris Crutcher.
p. cm.
Includes bibliographical references.
ISBN 0-325-00710-1 (alk. paper)
1. Kittle, Penny.   2. Teachers—United States—Biography.
3. Teaching—Anecdotes.   I. Title

LA2317.K557 A3 2005
370'.92—dc22   2005006624

EDITOR: *Lois Bridges*
PRODUCTION: *Lynne Costa*
COVER AND INTERIOR DESIGN: *Jenny Jensen Greenleaf*
COVER AND INTERIOR PHOTOGRAPH: *Ted Ostrem*
TYPESETTER: *Gina Poirier*
MANUFACTURING: *Louise Richardson*

Printed in the United States of America on acid-free paper
09 08 07 06 05 DA 1 2 3 4 5

dedicated with love to my parents
Ted and Barbara Ostrem
great storytellers, great teachers

Hope begins in the dark,
the stubborn hope that if you just show up
and try to do the right thing,
the dawn will come.
You wait and watch and work: you don't give up.

—ANNE LAMOTT

contents

foreword

once wrote a poem about a friend who died in Vietnam. After I read it aloud to a writing group, one group member said, "That's what I like to see—write about the tough stuff."

That's what Penny Kittle has done in *The Greatest Catch*. The students she writes about—students spanning the K–12 spectrum—you don't often see on the cover of books about teaching. But these troubled students are among those who have stuck with Penny over the years, the ones who rise to consciousness twenty years after their lives touched hers. Some of these students rejected school values and defied the system they found themselves in. Many of these students were grievously damaged. Some lived with an alcoholic parent or had been abused. Some were bright but stymied by formal educational assessments that arrived at a number but lost the person. Some were coming through slaughter and surviving the only way they could. Some had given up. Some kept slugging. Penny looks at these students as the ones that got away, the ones whose emotional lives were not improved by her care, no matter how hard she pushed, no matter how well she taught. I've been there. You have, too.

Despite the obstacles these students faced, despite the things they carried, *The Greatest Catch* is about hope. Many of these students had strength and resilience. And there was Mrs. Kittle meeting them every day in the classroom, putting her heart and mind to work, seeking to reach every one of them, especially the wounded ones who had constructed walls around themselves, blocking harm, blocking help, blocking hope.

Penny Kittle does this constant reaching out because she knows what the teaching commitment means. Here is a quotation from *The Greatest Catch* that I will place at the top of the syllabus for my undergraduates preparing to teach English:

> When you're teaching you're going to see people who cut corners, don't work as hard as they should, or just complain all the time about everything. I believe you've got to do what's right, every single day of your life, even if the rest of the crowd isn't. Teaching is about honor and goodness and mercy. It really is. And no one will be watching you most of the time. You either live up to the calling of the profession or you don't, and most likely no one will ever know but you. But it matters because the kids are counting on you.

I know there are teachers like Penny Kittle all over America. I meet them at writing workshops, presentations, and conferences. I teach them in graduate courses. I work with them as undergraduates before they become teachers. These accomplished teachers and teachers-to-be, though, don't always write their stories of teaching and learning as Penny Kittle has done here. I urge them to do so. I give them plenty of "you oughtas."

"You oughta tell the story of that student."

"You oughta write about that indelible teaching moment."

"That's the first line of a poem you've got there. You oughta finish it."

To aid readers in achieving their "you oughtas," Penny has written "craft notes" for some of the pieces in this volume. She shows how both patience and diligence enable writing to grow. She shows how dramatic scenes can anchor an essay and provide an indispensable structure, "like a life raft in a rolling ocean." Her craft notes, her insight about how to get writing done, will help and inspire you and your students.

Penny knows that writing is about more than spelling and punctuation. It is about more than summarizing and persuading. Writing is the great tool for developing our intellectual and emotional lives. In telling the story of a high school senior struggling gamely to write about her dying mother, Penny writes, "Writing can help you claw your way through a tragedy. Writing releases pain and often brings hope. Meaning is found. Not answers, but strength to continue."

In *The Greatest Catch* Penny Kittle has found meaning for her life in teaching, and that gives her strength to continue. She has answers in this book, too, answers that continue to sustain her and compel her to keep reaching. Read Penny's stories of teaching and learning. Then write your own. I plan to.

—*Tom Romano*

introduction

water and dawn and bait

*Angling teaches patience and grace, a silent communion
with the countryside and its creatures.*

—MARK KINGWELL

*I*t was dark, middle-of-the-night dark, when we hopped
down the bank to a bend in the Nahalem River. The air
caught in my lungs, so cold I became a bit more awake
with every quick breath. I watched my feet and swung my pole over
shrubs, trying to keep up with my agile and anxious father. He was in
the stream by the time I reached the bank, wading out with strong
strides into the heart of the river, tying the lure as he stumbled across
the river bottom, pausing only to secure a knot and break the end of
the line with his teeth, before he flung a look back at me as he cast
across water to a dark hole beneath a tree.

"There's where they are, hiding in that hole," he said calmly,
glancing at my rod as if to say, "Come on, already."

I selected a lure and a little weight for my line, tying awkwardly,
with the rhythmic spin, snap, and plunk of my father's casts reminding me of all the fishing going on while I was assembling gear. Later,

as the ice gathered on my line and my fingers froze, I watched the gray light of dawn begin to ease its way between us.

My father caught a beautiful steelhead that morning and I caught nothing but trees across the river with my errant casts. I loved the trying, though. There was the weight of my rod in my right hand and the feel of the line running against my index finger as it uncoiled from my reel and floated toward fish. A warm sweater, grey dawn, and Dad and I in love with the water made a sweet harmony in life I continue to seek.

And then I became a teacher.

And it was a lot like fishing.

I got my gear together and leapt into a stream, one and then another, learning the uniqueness of each fishing hole as I worked in six states and with such very different fish. From third graders all the way up to graduate students, the fishing lessons kept surprising me. The teachers who have what I want—a deep sense of mission, joy, energy, passion—understand that teaching is about more than content knowledge and lesson plans, just as fishermen know fishing is about more than what you catch. Some of these lessons I learned in my first few weeks on the job, and some I'm just coming to understand twenty years later, but they all help me see teaching as the gift it is. This book isn't about fishing, but there's a mysterious synchronicity between these two loves in my life that I've come to treasure. Long ago I figured out that the greatest catch was not the fish.

Here's a little of what else I've learned:

Lots of times you can go home after working all day with nothing to show for it, but you're still up early and ready to go on the next. Something calls to you and makes you want to get back on the water and try again. That happens time and again in teaching. The kids wear me out by the end of the day, but when the alarm rings I can't wait to be with them again.

You can fish your whole life and still get outplayed on a particular day.

When you're new you don't know what to buy to stock your tackle box, so you rely on others and borrow. Good fishermen share. Bad ones scowl at you and tell you to stay away from their spot on the bank. They hover over their stuff. Keep away from them.

A fish might make a beautiful show of the fight, leaping out of the water showing off, and you've got to just keep on pulling, because if you tire too easily, he's got you.

Silence is downright marvelous when you're fishing. And the silence that descends on my classroom when students wrap their whole selves around paperback books is a calm, settled place in a life of clatter and distraction.

Someone comes along to enforce the rules only rarely, so it's up to individuals to do what's right. Like when I used to fish with my dad at Bonneville Dam in Oregon. There would be all of these people catching sturgeon. We knew the rule: you only keep ones that are no smaller than three feet and no bigger than six feet, but people were breaking this rule all the time. I fumed watching them haul in a huge sturgeon that should be left, then clubbing it and taking it with them. No one would stop them. When you're teaching you're going to see people who cut corners, don't work as hard as they should, or just complain all the time about everything. I believe you've got to do what's right, every single day of your life, even if the rest of the crowd isn't. Teaching is about honor and goodness and mercy. It really is. And no one will be watching you most of the time. You either live up to the calling of this profession or you don't, and most likely no one will ever know but you. But it matters because the kids are counting on you.

Most people don't get at all what it means to fish—and you can't explain. There are all of these fine points to the art that outsiders can't understand. All they want to know is, "Did you catch anything?" "How big was it?" As if that is why we're on the river in the first place.

It's easy to lose track of time on the water.

The more I learn, the more I see, the more I want to cast again.

Fishermen are suspicious of those who have really orderly tackle boxes and clean, pressed fishing vests. How you organize your stuff is never as important as how you fish.

The weirdest things can work for bait—like Rice Krispy treats at South Twin Lake in central Oregon one summer. We were hauling in trout, one after another, and laughing so hard I thought my buddy Tom would fall out of the boat. Only those few who were beside me that day and saw it really believe that story. Wondrous things happen all the time in teaching and no one will see but you. It's a pity, but it's also a secret and wonderful truth.

When the line is in the water, others nearby are supposed to do their thing without disturbing me or my fish. I get mighty testy when I'm interrupted while teaching.

At the bottom of the tackle box is this old lure that worked once and never again, but you keep it near just in case. You never know when you're going to need it, but when you do, you'll be glad you hung on to it. It's why teachers are such pack rats, by the way.

My fishing buddies are friends for life. They understand something deep and mysterious about water and dawn and bait.

It seemed like every time Dad came by my spot on the bank to watch me fish, I couldn't do anything. Suddenly I couldn't cast; I snagged up all the time; I was a nervous wreck. I did my best fishing when it was just me and the fish. That's sure been true in teaching.

Sometimes I hook a fish and think I'm in control until it takes off, leaving my reel spinning in my hands. Never underestimate the strength and resolve of a fish to get away.

Never.

Fishing looks easy, but is actually so complex—you need to know how to play the line against your thumb, for example—but no one sees what you're doing, so they think you're just standing there.

The fish makes the run for open water and snaps the line. Even if you're using all the skill possible to coax it in, you'll be blamed for not keeping that fish on your line; it's just the way it is. You're going to have to get used to it.

A school of fish can be so captivating and rare, so slippery and crafty, so beautiful and strong, so brave and resilient, that one can make a life out of following them.

And never get bored.

And never wear out.

It's one of God's miracles.

There are rivers all over this country, winding near hills I'll never see, but I know they are spotted with fishermen out trying hard early in the morning. We are kin—though we've never met. I'd like to share a few secrets I've learned about trout and gear and the ones that got away. Gather near and let me tell you a few of my stories.

beginning

*Our greatest problems in life come not so much
from the situations we confront as from
our doubts about our ability to handle them.*

—SUSAN TAYLOR

There were just so many of them; thirty-four little faces in rows looking at me, dark hair, blonde hair, skin in several colors, and tiny little white teeth like Tic-Tacs in rows as they smiled and waved at me. "Good morning, third graders," I said with a big smile. I was charmed by their clean first-day-of-school clothes, sharpened pencils, and eagerness. They were darn cute, but I was nervous. How was I ever going to learn all of their names? I moved from one thing to the next, smiling and walking back and forth in front of the chalkboard, my hands fluttering as I checked my watch. My first day crawled along. We had another hour until recess; Lord, help me.

And then Kenny started giggling at Ryan. This sweet little boy in the front row wasn't listening. He poked his friend and raised his eyebrows when I explained our classroom rules. I scowled at him and started in on my next thing, figuring a lull in the action was the problem. He kept giggling, his shoulders bouncing up and down, dimples creased delightedly.

Uh oh.

I really hadn't expected it, especially not on my first day. I was taller than all of them, but that hadn't scared them. I scowled. The whole class giggled in response. I looked out from behind my scared blue eyes and saw a room of snickering little demons. My heart pounded a background tempo. What if I really couldn't do this?

"Shhh!" Short and sharp like a muffled sneeze, I shushed him. I'm not even sure where I learned that; it just came.

Kenny shook his straight brown hair a little and looked at Ryan and a few others nearby as he grinned broadly. He shrugged his shoulders at the class, then turned to look innocently back at me.

Now I was in trouble.

I flashed another mean teacher look, my eyes little slits of fury. "Please don't laugh while I'm talking, Kenny," I said it in the best serious teacher voice I could manage, each syllable distinct, with a decided hint of *don't-make-me-hurt-you.*

He stopped laughing. Just like that.

Excellent. I started breathing again and we made it to recess.

During my break I thought hard about little Kenny. I had ten minutes to figure him out. It wasn't even lunch on my first day of school and I was getting played by an eight-year-old. I wanted to knock my head against the chalkboard. Here I was in the California desert, twenty-one years old and barely past graduation day, beginning my career in a year-round school system. This land was a foreign country: sand blew across the playground; there were black widows in my house and a scorpion in my bathtub one morning; I'm not kidding. And then just days before school started, the district changed my teaching assignment from sixth grade to third, which meant my new students were just one week from the end of their second-grade year, and I knew nothing about seven- and eight-year-olds. Clearly. This entire situation made me feisty, come to think of it. I steamed. This was better than crying.

I admit it; I hoped Kenny would fall and scrape something so he wouldn't come back after recess. I know, not very teacherlike, was it? That nurturing thing was gone; the sniggering shake of his shoulders had done it. You're not supposed to be mad at children barely as tall as your waist, but this little guy had me. In five minutes he'd be back. I had to think of something.

It seemed that Kenny's friend Ryan was egging him on. I looked at the rows of empty desks and imagined the little people that had just left. Jennifer: dark helmet head of curls, glasses, starched blue dress, prim, disapproving smile. She didn't even grin when Kenny started in, unlike her classmates whose little eyes danced as they covered their mouths with their chubby fingers. That was it: I'd swap one Ryan for one Jennifer and be back in the driver's seat. And yes, I felt this little twinge of guilt for Jennifer as I lugged Kenny's desk next to hers, but this was a desperation maneuver, divinely inspired; you understand.

I heard the bell followed by the rumbling of feet as students raced across the pavement outside. I swallowed hard and went to the front of the room, *Stuart Little* in one hand, a piece of chalk in the other. I took a deep breath. I even took on a cowboy stance, one hand on each hip. C'mon y'all; let's see what you've got.

I waited.

I heard only the wind outside my door. I could hear classrooms starting up on all sides of me, but where were my students? Surely all thirty-four hadn't ended up in the nurse's office; that was too much to hope for. (Thirty-three would be enough, actually. I'd take Jennifer back.) I went to the door and looked across the empty playground. The wind whipped up little dust storms on the empty playground. Finally I peeked around my portable to the large open fields. In a line at the center of the baseball diamond were three dozen little bodies and one crabby playground aide with a whistle in her hand looking straight at me.

I darted back behind the door, but I knew she'd seen me. Oops. I hustled toward my class. "I'm sorry; I thought they came back to the room after recess; I didn't know I was supposed to come and get them," I called as I got closer, the wind whipping my long hair into jagged little spikes. Her dark glasses reflected my desperate face. She looked at me carefully for a minute. Her lips formed a straight line.

"Did you go over the rules with your class before you let them out this morning?" Her tone was crisp, crackling a little as it met that fierce desert wind.

"Oh, no, whoops." Somebody snickered in line. I tried that mean squint, but the sun was blinding me.

"I'm sorry," I offered.

"Well, these two"—she motioned at Kenny and Ryan, now sitting in the dirt beside her—"are going to spend the next few
recess periods as My Little Helpers. They need to be reminded of
the r-u-l-e-s." The boys rolled their eyes at each other and smiled
at me.

"Yes, of course, we'll do that; thank you," I was already moving
away. I tried to keep from smiling at our collective guilt as we walked
in a silent and perfectly straight line all the way to our door. We were
united in fear. She was still watching us when I motioned the children in our door and quickly shut it behind me.

"All right, you little darlings, time to go over the R-U-L-E-S," I
said with a scowl. There was a serious silence in reply. I looked at
those frozen faces and thought, *I can do this.* "But first we're going to
read. Find a book and a place and get settled." I smiled.

I ignored Kenny's resentful scowl as he squirmed into his new
seat, inching his chair away from Jennifer. I held out a book on baseball. "Do you play?" I asked him.

He relaxed a little, said, "Yeah," and reached for it. I'd win this kid
over; I was sure of it.

There was reading and math to carry us into lunchtime and then
we were lining up again, on the move. I watched my students march
before me to the cafeteria with lunch boxes and brown paper sacks
swinging in time, a long line of children I was responsible for. I had
one girl on each side holding my hands: Kristina chattering about her
little brother, Joey, born just weeks before; Sandra silently running
her fingers across the back of my hand, huddled close. They made
room for me at their table and the others practically sat on top of
each other to be near me. My peanut butter sandwich had never
tasted as sweet.

I walked back to my portable classroom giddy with the love of the
work, ready to prepare for the afternoon. The sun warmed my shoulders, the hills all around the school were a dusty blue, beautiful and
serious. The background music was laughter and a child hollering,
"Hi, Miss Ostrem!" from the four-square game.

I felt my place in a foreign land.

I was a teacher.

Ilearned everything the hard way my first year, I swear. I gave out no homework for weeks and then when the kids complained I gave out far too much, prompting parents to come storming to my door. I planned a field trip to Disneyland of all places, and then lost a group of kids when the central office administrator I borrowed as a chaperone let them have some "free time." (You think I'm making this up; trust me, it happened.) I moved in and out of my classroom every nine weeks for our rotating year-round schedule and got to know the night janitors well because there was always more to do, more to learn. I loved every bit of it. But what stays in my mind are two scenes from spring.

After our April vacation my students were brimming with stories. They knew I had traveled back to Oregon for the holiday and were eager to hear about my trip. I suggested we act out something we had done and the others could guess.

Danny began. He loved going first. His lurches and jumps showed him playing soccer. The hands waved across the room.

"Eddy," he called. Boys always call on their best friends; it must be a secret pact or something.

"Soccer!"

"Yep, and we won the whole tournament!" he beamed.

The class burst into applause.

"Congratulations, Danny, very cool," I said. "You call on the next person."

He smiled broadly and turned to point his finger at me, "Miss Ostrem!" More cheers. You gotta love it; I can't think of another place in my life where crowds applaud when it's my turn to talk.

I brought two fingers of my right hand together and slowly moved them down my left ring finger. Mouths dropped open and hands waved as Amy yelled, "You're getting married!"

"Yes," I laughed. "I got engaged to Mr. Kittle, the one you met a few months ago when he came to visit." The room exploded in noise.

"When are you getting married?" Ryan shouted.

"We don't know yet," I said quietly, shushing my class and watching Michael's hand still waving from the back of the room. Little Michael Heywood—I adored him. He had round, dark-framed glasses and a huge crush on me. He was eager to get my attention.

"Michael?"

"What was it like?" The other kids squealed, calling out "yeah, tell us!" as Michael continued, "Did he just say," and he dropped ceremoniously to one knee as he spoke, "'Miss Ostrem, will you marry me?' just like that?" He batted the long eyelashes across his brown eyes as the kids hooted around him.

Thirty-four eager smiles waited for my answer.

"Well, almost," I said. "He calls me Penny, though, not Miss Ostrem."

"He *does*?" More open mouths and hysterical giggles.

But of course, the news also meant I would be moving at the end of the school year. Pat had work in Oregon and I wanted to be with him. I stuffed our scrapbook and my posters and projects and homemade math games into one cardboard box and then another. I filled my rusty Dodge Swinger to the very brim with boxes each night. The walls were stripped of cheerful student stories and I met my replacement one afternoon at the copy machine, but I still don't think *leaving* sank in until I walked to the door of my classroom at the end of our last day of school and turned to face those familiar rows of smiling faces. Ryan's face was flushed; Jennifer's bottom lip quivered; Kristina held the tissue box in one hand and a card she'd made in the other.

My eyes suddenly overflowed.

I tried to say, "I have loved being your teacher and I'll miss you so much," as the first few stepped forward to give me a hug, but I was lost in tears. I realized they would grow up without me and I would never see most of them again. Ever. I ran my fingers through Ronnie's hair and told him to take care of his younger sister. I held Sandra against me a little longer than the others. I didn't think I could let them go; I knew I couldn't say how much their love and trust had helped me learn how to be a teacher. I silently bent down to hug each one as they went out the door. I didn't stop sniffling until far north of Hesperia.

I couldn't get over the wonder of this work with children.

Twenty years later, I still can't.

my first steelie

Hope burns always in the heart of the fisherman.
—ZANE GREY

In November the run of fish is legendary in Oregon, and I get anxious to be on the water. I am serious about steelhead. It came from following my father over weathered wood fences through cow pastures at dawn looking for just the right bend in the Wilson River. It came from watching him hook a monster once, fifty-two pounds, and slowly bring her to shore while I stood holding the net. It came from falling in love with a man in college who loved the water as much as I did. I followed him from one elegant spot to the next, but came home empty-handed every time. Somehow it didn't feel that way, though. Time on the water is never wasted time.

Fishing once meant time with my father away from expectations, awkward conversations, and memories of our past. As my education surpassed his, he seemed to pick fights with me, challenging my understanding of local politics or history, leaving me frustrated. On the river he was the undisputed authority, always, and we both breathed easier. He knew the right hook, fly, or line to use depending on the time of year, the rain, or his instincts. I loved the sound of him rooting around in his tan tackle box, a mess of bobbers, weights, flat plastic spools of colored line, and neon yarn bits. Hooks in tiny plastic cases littered the bottom shelf, tiny capsules of round, grey lead in containers with red twisty tops lay near wire cutters for tangled line, and there was usually a pack of matches, the cover warped from water that inevitably found its way into the box. Dad had a solution to every fishing frustration; he whistled Roger Miller tunes as he tossed things aside.

Fishing is waiting, and although in the rest of my life I'm pretty impatient, I will wait for fish. It is an opportunity to be out in the air, watching the wind in the trees and the ever changing surface of a stream as it gathers in pools or spills around the sides of a rock. You stand in hip waders and feel the tug—the force of all that water against your legs—and you are part of the river, never mind if you catch anything. I've always craved the silence of fishing—the anticipation—the surprise and wonder of a fish swimming by my line and opening its mouth for a taste. In November I hum with that expectation, dreaming of a dark ride down an empty highway in layers of cotton and wool, a Thermos of hot black coffee between my hands.

I can feel fishing in the chill of November, in the clouds that circle my head when I exhale, and in my memories of Jerry. I sometimes think now that fishing saved him, the way it had fed me life when I needed it, but I'm not sure about that. I do know it changed something in both of us.

Jerry had blond, kind of greasy hair that clung below his eyebrows, almost across his tense blue eyes. He was chubby and, I suspect, wore whatever clothes were on the floor from the day before. Jerry was dismissive of adults, uninterested in my conversation. He was in my remedial math class the first hour on that first day of eighth grade. I had naively agreed to leave my fifth-grade classroom behind and take an opening in the upper grades, just to try something new. It was early in my career, but I already loved jumping grade levels like hurdles, feeling yards ahead of my colleagues stuck in place. Jerry, however, was unimpressed from the start. He folded his plump arms across his chest and said with steely conviction, "You can't make me."

Jerry sat bemused in math class and then returned after lunch for remedial English. I was dismayed when he came through my door again late in the afternoon for homeroom. Someone had ordered up three doses of Jerry a day for me, and I was sure I was allergic. The child who sat doing nothing—no doodling, no spitballs, no talking, and certainly no work—in both math and English, was now going to do nothing in homeroom. How should I play this fish? He didn't move like the others I'd known. I was new to teaching adolescents and I just hadn't accumulated enough stuff in my tackle box yet; I needed more time on the water with a master before they put me out in the river by myself. I asked colleagues about Jerry, but they didn't suggest another lure or more weight on my line—they told me to move on to another fishing hole. They'd been after him for years with no luck.

This was against my nature. Fishermen don't just walk away; they reel in and cast again.

I was friendly, but Jerry ignored me. I approached. He didn't budge. Reel in; snag. I suggested getting started; he smirked. He was fourteen. The school had tried retention already; Jerry was not going to do it. If you tested him, he'd know it all—I was sure of it. There was an intellect below his dull look, but he wouldn't let us see. He'd pick up a pencil and write in miniature letters of perfect grey script an intriguing answer to a question, and I'd think, "Excellent! I've set the hook..." but he was either toying with me or just plain bored, because his folded arms returned minutes later.

Our best times were during homeroom, because there was nothing to learn, no questions to be answered, just help if you wanted it and a place to hang out until the final bell rang. Jerry watched me help Trina, with the wild red curls and the spelling deficiency. His eyes followed me when I moved to sit beside his only friend, encouraging him, coaching him, and joking with him. Jerry looked at me when I handed him missing assignment notices from other teachers: little slips of white paper in a pile at his desk, still there after chairs were put up, coats zipped, and students gone, but he silently shook his head when I suggested he get started. Jerry's father said that was just Jerry. He appreciated my interest, but Jerry pretty much did as he pleased; he didn't expect me to change him. Mom had left when the boys were little—before kindergarten—and Jerry had just never had much of an interest in school.

So Jerry and I kept our distance as fishermen space themselves along a bank, close enough to watch, but careful not to get in each other's way. At the end of first quarter Jerry's grade point average was 0.6, his D– in PE keeping him from the cellar. Jerry smirked, then crumpled the report in his right fist, not bothering to aim it for the wastebasket; he let it fall from his hand and roll to the edge of his desk. It felt like my failure as well as his. I was frustrated. With Dad beside me I always felt smarter than the fish; with Jerry I surely wasn't. It was my job to help, so I got a little more aggressive the following week. I pulled up a seat beside him every day to talk. It reminded me of fly casting with my father in the backyard years ago, willing my line to float like his, sending it out again and again and again until darkness forced us inside.

As second quarter began, two things happened at once. Trina started taunting me to match her one-on-one in basketball and I agreed. Homeroom emptied to gather outside in the cool stillness of November, all fourteen of them cheering for Trina as I lunged and darted around her, sinking most of my shots. By the time the buses pulled in I was up by ten. That competitive side has always been a bit of a problem for me; I can be such a jerk when I'm winning. I bugged the bystanders, "Who's next?" and my eyes lit on Jerry. I was talking before I even thought about it, another persistent character flaw of mine.

"Jerry," I grinned.

"I don't play basketball, Ms. Kittle," he said, shaking his head as our eyes locked.

"I know; that's not what I was thinking. We"—I motioned to our homeroom and they closed in around us in a circle—"all know that you're smart. You just won't let anybody see. So I challenge you," and I put my finger out, pointing right at his chest, "to make the honor roll second quarter."

The class roared.

"I have no question in my mind that you can, but there are a lot of people in this school who wouldn't believe it. I want you to: Prove. Them. Wrong." I turned away, sending a jump shot at the hoop, a perfect swish that seemed to seal the deal. Slick maybe, but my insides were churning. Was this the right thing to do?

What he said was, "I don't care about honor roll," but what I saw was interest. I had hope. Jerry sauntered off to the school bus and boarded with the rest, taking a seat near the window in the back. I felt an invisible line between us, fragile, but sure.

And then that very next week: fishing class. Big River was right outside our back door and when the principal suggested we pilot elective courses for six weeks I volunteered to teach the kids how to cast. I was bouncing from heel to toe just thinking about it. A colleague with more seniority jumped at my idea, though, and I was left to cover study hall. Yeah, I was disappointed, but I accepted that rookies took the crummy jobs and the older teachers got what they wanted. I went by fishing class frequently, however, peeking in the door hoping someone needed my help. Sitting up front, every single day, eyes on his teacher, was Jerry. Finally we had something to talk about. He brought his favorite flies to show me after school, gradually letting me share my fishing stories and even photographs of my greatest catches. Jerry learned the essentials of fishing quickly, and told me school was finally teaching him something he could use. Our elective courses made all of our work richer, because kids are different on the water or when quietly clicking knitting needles. And so are teachers.

As winter shortened our days, Jerry became more compliant. He brought a new energy to class. He did work during homeroom and the pile of white slips announcing his missing assignments disappeared. Fish on. I hoped he was taking me up on my honor roll challenge, but I didn't mention it, afraid to put pressure on him, afraid to ruin the casual comfort we had found in talking about silver salmon and the search for the perfect cast. I watched him often that December, and when our eyes met, he smiled. No teeth, but a grin and a softening around his eyes.

I squealed when I held Jerry's second quarter report card in my hand—his lowest grade was a C in science. We cheered him in homeroom and I promised to make cupcakes in his honor that night. Weeks later at our winter awards assembly the principal recognized Jerry's rise—the largest grade point jump he'd ever seen—with a nod toward me, his homeroom teacher. Jerry didn't seem to mind, and perhaps I'd earned a little of the credit, but I don't believe I was the real magic in what had happened.

I can still see Jerry in a line of students at the front of the stage as the principal leaned into the microphone and then bent over to shake Jerry's hand. Jerry had on a red shirt and jeans, his bangs were still hanging across his eyes, and he looked out at the audience of clapping hands with a smug but cautious pride. I thought his father should see it, but he didn't attend the assembly that day.

When third quarter began, Jerry went back to noncompliance. The grades were not a reward he sought, the things we taught seldom of interest to him. He stopped trying. And it hurt because I knew in the hands of a skilled fisherman he'd probably have come all the way to shore. Jerry failed eighth grade and then ninth. The summer he turned sixteen sealed it. He never returned to school in the fall. I heard he went to work at the paper mill down the road; by now he's probably married with his own children. I wonder sometimes if he's still fishing. I still drool a little when I drive by a bend in the river and see a few scattered fishermen straight and still in the water, their rods in a line against the current, waiting. I slow the car and watch them, tempted to slide along beside them. And yes, I call myself a fisherman, even though these days the closest I get is eating red gummy fish at the movie theatre in town.

Fishing is in my blood for life. Each September I head back to school after Labor Day. I feel the force of all that water rushing by me, standing in my hip waders trying to catch fish. My father's voice reminds me to be patient and learn the ways of the fish first. I try. I even hook a steelhead now and then, holding it on my line just long enough to watch it flash in the sunlight. If I'm lucky, I can keep it on and gradually bring it to shore after a tremendous battle, but too many these days break free and disappear from sight.

Penny

I have come to a frightening conclusion. I am the decisive element in the classroom. It is my personal approach that creates the climate. It is my daily mood that makes the weather. As a teacher I possess the tremendous power to make a child's life miserable or joyous. I can be a tool of torture or an instrument of inspiration. I can humiliate or humor, hurt or heal. In all situations it is my response that decides whether a crisis will be escalated or de-escalated, and a child humanized or de-humanized.

—DR. HAIM G. GINOTT

*I*t was my sixth birthday and there I was in first grade with that little, mean Mrs. Brockson and those long, long rows of desks all the way to the front where she stood with a spindly, pointed stick and her roll-up map. She had a black dress and black shoes, and small, black-framed glasses that reflected so I couldn't even see her eyes. She was so important it made me tremble just to watch her. I was in my new dress that Mother had sewn for me and I felt the bumps of seersucker against my smooth palms as I ran them across my legs.

I took a quick breath and swallowed. It was a long walk to the front and the lines around her mouth deepened as I came forward.

My shoes made too much noise on that shiny floor and I slowed to quiet them. It made me have to pee even more, watching her watching me as I stepped to the front. There were wrinkles in my dress from sitting, my stringy hair was messy, the hole in my right shoe, bothersome. She must see all my faults.

I stood before her and the words wouldn't come. She leaned forward slightly as I stammered, a disappointed frown at her lips and dark, hairy eyebrows rising above her glasses. As she understood me she straightened up, and with a toss of her dark head of curls said distinctly, "Not now." Clean, crisp, and efficient, Mrs. Brockson dismissed me and returned her attention to the papers on her desk, moving them around a bit as I pivoted to return to my desk.

Not now, but when?

I watched my shoes move in and out of sight as I returned to my seat, feeling the eyes of all the children in class on me. A startling, insistent bell rang and she began talking of something, or several somethings, so far up front in that quiet room. The room stilled to listen— white walls, polished linoleum floors, and those mysterious ceiling tiles above with tiny holes lined up in rows. One long blackboard stretched across the front, cold and clean, still marked by vertical streaks from the janitor's sponge. The date was printed in tight cursive in the right corner. I looked at Mrs. Brockson and tried not to think about holding it. Mrs. Brockson must think I'm grown up, I smiled to myself, remembering that six was so much older than boring old five. I swung my feet wildly beneath my seat, a strong rhythm that helped me hold on.

I felt my dress; Mom made this. The hem was perfectly straight, small stitches in red thread. I remembered her hemming as we watched *The Mary Tyler Moore Show,* Mom's favorite, the night before. I was sure it wouldn't be finished to wear to school today and went to bed not knowing, Mom's eyes squinting into thin lines as she passed the needle through bunches of fabric carefully pinned together. I liked watching my mom when she didn't know I was. I liked the short black line she drew at the outside corner of her eyes almost like a longer, untamed eyelash. Her teased hair surrounded her head like a cloud of airy brown curls. Mom was always doing.

Mrs. Brockson signaled to the class and chairs pushed back around me as my classmates stood. I scrambled to join them, placing my right hand across my chest and turning toward the small flag propped near the door. But the minute I was on my feet I felt the rush, the insistent need to go NOW. I clenched my fists and my eyes tight as I fought this urge and began to murmur with my classmates, "I pledge allegiance. . . ." I would have bent over if I could. I felt sick.

A stream started down my left leg and I struggled to shut it off, rocking from one foot to the other. I felt my white ankle sock soaked against my shoe and still it ran over the lip of my shoe, forming a puddle beneath me. There was a brief moment when I thought it would stop, that I might be able to conceal it under a book, but the stream was followed by a torrent as the students chanted, "one nation, under God," and all was lost. I looked down at the pale yellow river I'd created against that gleaming floor. A thin stream headed toward the empty seats behind me.

Andy saw it first. He was in the row next to me, just ahead, and something made him glance back as he spoke, eyes widening at the puddle below me, smile filling his face as he removed his hand from his chest and pointed at the floor. "Mrs. Brockson!" he alerted her just as silence followed the pledge, "Penny has wet her pants!" Andy shrieked with excitement as the students nearby leapt to their feet again. A chorus of chaos followed in rapid succession: "Ooo! My shoes! Yuck!" I stood staring at the floor, my face hot, and tears dropped from my cheeks to splash into the yellow puddle I'd created.

I felt Mrs. Brockson call, "For goodness' sakes!", barely suppressing her rage; I saw her nostrils flare as her mouth became a sneer. I was thankful then that I couldn't see her eyes. I felt the collapse of all I had hoped to do in first grade: have my teacher like me, show her how smart I was, make her smile. I felt the name-calling that would follow me for several years. I was a bad kid. I had peed all over her beautiful floor. And I had ruined my birthday dress.

It was official now: I really was the little baby. When I had entered kindergarten the year before, I was the only four-year-old in the room, once Julia turned five on our very first day of school. The other kids called me a baby-baby, some boasting that they would be six before I even turned five! I should go home to Mama, they'd giggle, and I agreed with them. But we were in a dark year and my home was a confusing, tough place. There was drinking and sobering up and messes to clean. As a bright and capable child, anxious to please her mother, I'm sure I convinced her I was ready to go; after all, Julia was. But I hated being the youngest every year, every class in school. Thirteen when I entered high school, years later, and then the last one to drive. And far more important, as was evident that day in Mrs. Brockson's room, I was a little confused, a little socially behind my classmates. I was always the last to get the joke. I suppose it is understandable that my first real love had skipped a grade in elementary school and was even six months younger than I when we met in college.

There's a jumble of images that finish that day—sitting in the main office in cold, damp clothes, waiting for my mother, avoiding the eyes of the secretary. The warmth I felt when Mom came through the door at last, a bag of clothes in one hand, and her forgiving smile causing my tears to start again. I finished the day somehow in the clothes Mom had brought from home. I spent my birthday in complete silence, forming letters upon a page, drumming my fingers like twin spiders on the cream-colored cement wall at recess, chewing little of my lunch at a table alone, avoiding everyone's eyes.

Sitting beside Mom, looking over the dashboard as we drove home that afternoon, I watched the trees lead us home. She cheerfully sang along with Wayne Newton on the radio. We passed my sister, walking home with Cammie and Cathy, and I shrank below the window edge. No doubt she had heard by now and would share her disgust with me later. Mom finally lapsed into silence and we pulled the car near the curb below our house.

I got out silently, heard the familiar thud as I shut the door behind me and climbed the steps toward home. Butchie bounded forward, blond ears flapping, tags jingling from his collar, eyes delighted that I had arrived. Unconditional love: I felt it with assurance for the first time, perhaps. Felt it in my dog, in my mother who never said a word to reprimand me, in the welcoming windows of our white house as I drew near. School would remain a place of trial for years, but I had places and people that loved me, forgave me, and helped me move on.

My red plaid dress was clean and pressed within days. It hung in my closet, jinxed by its inaugural wearing, until it was too small for me to close the buttons down the back. I'm not sure I ever wore it again. The stain inside of me, however, took much longer to wash away.

Today, as a classroom teacher, I look back at this moment and remember how it felt to be one in a classroom of so many. I remember how little my teachers knew of my life. I pledge to be different—to notice, to care, to love my students even when their needs disrupt my plans, and always to say yes—now—go if you need to.

David

There were things for which it was impossible to prepare
but which one spent a lifetime looking back at,
trying to accept, interpret, comprehend.

—JHUMPA LAHIRI

*D*avid wasn't popular; he was entirely uncool. His head seemed larger than it needed to be, like it must be a challenge to keep his balance as he stumbled down the hall to my room. His bright blue eyes sat like marbles on the surface of his face and were always wide open. He smiled mysteriously to himself. His long arching forehead met a mass of dark, matted hair, and he was a giant next to every child in the school, but he didn't hunch his shoulders or cower near his friends; he skipped down the hall with his Bugs Bunny lunch box clanking beside him. He seemed thrilled with the attention he drew. "Hello!" he'd call loudly to children in the hall, bumping into the wall as his exuberant waving threw him off balance.

All of this shouldn't really matter in fifth grade, but of course it does.

"Time for science," I'd say. He'd hoot and clap his hands and start digging in his desk for his book. Science was so much fun! The other kids barely contained their snickers. David didn't mind, he'd mutter and sing to himself, patting his belly. He had a protruding stomach and his T-shirt stretched across it, leaving a band of pale, jiggly flesh near his waist. I hate to see overweight kids in ill-fitting clothes, but David loved to show us his "outie" belly button and chuckle as he rubbed his bare, round tummy. The other students covered their mouths to mostly suppress their giggles and rolled their eyes.

David tuned in and out of class as if he were in a giant pinball machine spinning from one thing to the next; he just wasn't *with* us. I remember during a health lesson I asked if anyone could show me where the skeletal muscles were. His hand shot up with an, "Oh! Oh! Oh!" and I hesitated, but called on him.

"I've got it," he shouted, "Sneezy, Sleepy, Dopey," counting on his fingers, "and Doc!" He nodded and applauded as if he were at the center of a celebration while my students shrieked in laughter. I remembered before school that day when a crowd of kids at my desk had tried to name all seven dwarfs and forgot four, but David didn't see how weird it was to shout this out during health hours later.

It seemed impossible for David to fit in.

I figured he was just odd, something I couldn't fix.

And then one day David was distressed over something he needed out of his desk to take to recess. I said I'd help him look. We tried digging at the mass that projected out the front, but it was so packed there was no way to see what was inside. David was increasingly troubled as I poked among his papers and couldn't find it. I told him we should just dump the mess onto the floor. He shouted, "Yeah, let's!" and clapped his hands loudly. One tip and there was a roar, followed by a tinkling avalanche of brown bottles, each with a perky yellow label that read Real Vanilla Flavoring. They hit the linoleum like bizarre gunfire, *ping, ping, tink, ping.*

Now, his desk was so full of crap that this didn't strike me as all that odd at first; collecting things was a typical fifth-grade behavior. They sat in this pile on the floor and I kept looking from David to the crumpled papers and half-chewed yellow pencils, wrappers, Matchbox cars, and wads of pale blue chewed gum with a perplexed look. How could one kid dig out from under all of this? There was a sour smell coming from old milk cartons and I suppressed a gag. And then I thought, why did he need so much vanilla flavoring? What in the world was this kid *baking*? And they were empty bottles. I shrugged it off, and picked up the stuff as the other kids went to recess. I had work to do.

At lunch I sat next to my buddy Nate, a veteran of many years who'd had David the year before, and we commiserated. "David's odd all right," I said, "but I like him. But get *this*—he's got vanilla flavoring bottles in his desk—like a dozen of them; I'm not kidding. We just cleaned it. Isn't that crazy? What do you think he's baking?"

Nate gave me a look—it was pity almost—like "how unfortunate to be so dim" and then he said slowly, "Uh, I think he's probably been *drinking* it, Penny. Vanilla flavoring is pretty concentrated alcohol."

I widened my eyes in a stupefied stare; I finally squeaked, "It is?" and swallowed the bite of soggy wheat bread and peanut butter down with a gulp. Nate absentmindedly stirred green peas in a congealing pool of gravy with his spoon. He still ate the school lunch every day no matter what they were serving. He smiled grimly and nodded. "You'd better tell the counselor; I think David's an alcoholic. In fact, I'd bet my lunch on it." We snickered morosely together. He continued, "You know, that would explain a lot from last year."

Nate was right. This ten-year-old had a drinking problem. No wonder every day was a party. I didn't think that happened in real classrooms, certainly not mine. We found empty cough syrup bottles in David's lunch box and more in the class trash can. Our guidance counselor spoke to the manager of the small store nearest the school and discovered a disturbing pattern of purchases, and more important, a recent disappearance of stock from the shelves that matched exactly what we had found at school.

As the information settled, one thought kept repeating: *you are in way over your head here.* I had no idea what this teaching work was all about; one look around my classroom confirmed it. I had pictured rows of pleasant children waiting for my gift of knowledge; instead I had giddy David watching his world spin by as I blathered on about multiplication. There was Darlene, with the abusive father, and Jim, who traveled to a different relative's house about every two weeks, leaving all of his things behind. I had strange and silent Stephen, who always smelled like urine. Exactly where was the teaching supposed to happen in this world of insanity? This wasn't about being a second-year teacher; this was the work. And I was completely outmatched.

I thought I was prepared when I left college, but I wasn't even close. We studied all of these cases in isolation and there seemed to be solutions. I knew about social problems and child psychology; they just hadn't shown me all of this tossed together in one classroom like a miserable potluck stew. And right beside the ones who desperately needed help were the ones who seemed to have normal home lives; they wore clean clothes and their parents picked them up on time. The homework got done; the kids were well-rested, respectful, and ready to learn; the parents returned my phone calls. I didn't think I could screw any of those kids up too badly. But should I focus my energy on their education or the calamity and desperation in the lives of the others? Certainly the work would be different. Since I felt responsible for both, how was I going to do it all at once?

I called David's parents and asked them to come in for a conference. Both worked at the paper mill on the swing shift, part of their regular rotating schedule. When they could fit me in two weeks later, the mother explained that "Tuesday is Saturday and Wednesday is my Sunday that week, so it looks like Sunday is our best bet. We'll see you on Wednesday." Suddenly I understood why David never could straighten out which day it was in school.

She heard my hesitation and laughed with a touch of condescension, saying, "You've never worked swing shift, have you?"

I admitted I hadn't.

She continued, "Well, it was much worse when David's dad and me were on different shifts. Then Monday was my Friday but his Sunday."

Hell, I was confused. Never mind David.

They arrived together and were happy to shake my hand; they said David was liking school this year. Mom had a Bud Light in one hand and a cigarette in the other, but I didn't confront her. It was after hours and the school was empty; I wasn't ready to challenge her. I looked at my notes and started with the discovery of the vanilla flavoring. When I explained that flavoring contained quite a bit of alcohol, Mom cut me off.

"Now, how exactly did you find these? You said you dumped out his desk onto the floor? I don't like that at all." She sat up straighter and tossed her long, dark hair over her shoulder with a sneer. She slapped the beer bottle against the desk with a decided clunk. I noticed the sweat forming on the bottle and at my hairline.

"I was trying to help," I stammered. "David was looking for a key chain or something he wanted."

"Well, I think that was his property and you shouldn't be in it," she continued. The father remained silent, arms crossed against his chest, leaning back in his chair. I could barely see his eyes underneath his black baseball hat.

I struggled to get our conference back on track; "I'm sorry. I—," but she interrupted again.

"I don't think I'm the one you should be apologizing to."

The conference didn't improve much over the next half hour. I tried to explain my fears and she talked around the issue, focusing instead on David's poor teachers in the past, his laziness, and their own low expectations for him because he seemed to be "a little slow." The disagreement hinged on the fact that I'd never seen him actually drinking anything. I figured my poor communication skills were the reason they weren't hearing me. It was a perfect disaster.

The bottom line: David continued to smuggle in alcohol in many surprising forms throughout his year in my classroom. I'm still not sure he even understood his bizarre cravings. In June he smiled broadly and gave me a happy high five to celebrate the end of the year, but even as I high-fived back I was conflicted; he was still in trouble. The counselor and I made recommendations, but David's parents had final say.

They said, "Stay out of this."

That year I began to master the art of instruction, but at times the rest of the work still leaves me reeling. I've come to accept this: I can't do it all. With two decades of teaching behind me, I now know where to find help for kids when they need it, how to deliver tough news to parents, and that I can depend on my colleagues to step in when I don't know what to do. I remember David and know that I could get him help today, help I just couldn't put my hands on in the hustle of being a new teacher. And I also know that chance will come again. Public schools draw all kids: it is the burden and the opportunity of teaching there.

grace

You will make all kinds of mistakes:
but as long as you are generous and true and also fierce
you cannot hurt the world or even seriously distress her.

—WINSTON CHURCHILL

I wasn't even a student teacher yet when I made my mark.
It was a practicum experience: a foray into the world of
teaching each morning, classes in the afternoon. Oregon
State was smart to put undergraduates into classrooms so quickly; it
allowed me to experience several grade levels by graduation as well as
several styles of teaching. But it also meant that I was only nineteen when
I met my first graders. Damn, they were cute. Damn, I was unprepared.

My mentor teacher was a confident professional, running in the
morning before work, arranging each day with this impressive balance of skill work and fun. The six-year-olds loved her and she loved
them. I hovered at the edge of the class, cutting out letters for the
bulletin board, finding lost jackets after recess, counting money for
the class book orders. I didn't have any real responsibility for the students, thank God. The closest I got was reading books to pairs of students. It was natural to ask questions, listen to their thinking, and
consider how I could help them learn strategies for figuring out the

pictures and words that worked together to make meaning. It felt like those essential, first, staggering baby steps for a teacher: learning how to talk to kids. I loved every minute of it.

Carl and Eddy liked me. They scrambled to grab my hand when it was reading time, always first in line. I knew that Elizabeth was disappointed when I read with the boys three days in a row, but there they were each day and I didn't know how to say no. By day five, Mrs. Simms stepped in. I needed to work with other kids in class. The day was brilliant with spring, warm and bright; she glanced outside and said I could take a small group to the empty playground and read with them. Many hands waved my way, but I chose Elizabeth, Angela, Kate, and Melissa to join the boys because they looked tame. I had a six-pack of bouncing, giggling children following me out the classroom door as I marched forward, tentatively in charge.

"Let's go to the logs by the bark dust," I called behind me as they cheered. In just those few moments my task compounded; my six students went in six directions. I looked for a place to sit comfortably in my skirt. As a few kids ran for the swings, I reached back to encourage two stragglers to join us.

"Come on, girls," I called, smiling at Kate and Melissa as they rushed forward with hands out to cling to each side of me. I kept walking, my hands outstretched, waiting to connect. Well, I connected all right. As I turned forward I went smack into the jungle gym at the edge of the playground. One bar was lined up perfectly with the bridge of my nose and I hit it with power. Imagine a Batman cartoon: Kabam!

I howled and bent over in pain, thinking I had broken my entire face. I pictured a horror show, blood squirting from my eyes, nightmare stuff. I could hear the gasps of the little ones running toward me. I couldn't open my eyes to see if they were all with me, but their excited little breaths felt like a group. "Miss Ostrem! Are you okay?" I heard Elizabeth's anxious voice. I sank to my knees; my eyes watered.

"She's dying!"

"She is?!"

"Oh," I whispered.

"Get Mrs. Simms!" Kate announced with authority.

I put out my hand: "No." I wanted to handle this, but speaking made my temples throb. "Wait. Just give me a minute," I whispered and tried to open my eyes.

As I began to focus between my fingers, I saw little faces peering up into mine, their eyes filled with concern. They were crouched in a circle waiting, their knees side by side in a knobby line. I struggled to regain my balance. I managed to sit on the log and my students clapped. Six-year-olds will celebrate anything. Elizabeth put the back of her hand against my forehead, saying seriously, "It doesn't feel like you have a fever." My students sat silently while I held my head and watched the bark dust spin beneath me.

Finally Melissa said, "Miss Ostrem, I could read *Curious George* if you want. I read it to my brother all the time."

I nodded.

She held the book before her and made sure we could see the pictures as she turned the pages.

Recess came. I went home to my apartment. Aspirin didn't help. When I finally visited the infirmary on campus that night, I discovered I'd broken my nose. By morning I had two purple-black eyes and a swollen face. My first visible teaching wound.

Now, instead of that being a freak accident, it turned out to be only the beginning. My husband calls me the absentminded professor, in fact. It seems grossly unfair: I'm *on* all the time as a teacher, juggling what I'm trying to accomplish with kids hour after hour, carrying in my head the ideas and plans and dreams for dozens of adolescents at once. This mind isn't absent. But then again, I kind of know what he means. I trip over stuff in the hall on my way to class that other people manage to maneuver around. I slide across the linoleum floor in my spikey-heeled black boots while trying to take attendance.

I run into desks while I'm teaching.

I fling pens at kids while I'm gesturing wildly.

I have tripped over the cord for the overhead projector more than once. I really have: arms flailing, papers flying, squeal escaping, face reddening. Guess we know why my parents didn't name me after family matriarch Grandma Grace.

This stuff seems to happen more often to me than to others I know. Last week I splattered black cartridge ink all over my face when I clapped my hands in excitement in the middle of a lesson. I'd forgotten that pen in my right hand. My seniors were wildly entertained. And there was Todd. "Nice, Kittle. Would you like me to get you a Kleenex?"

I soak my sleeve in coffee more than once a week. Or I dump the whole cup on my desk and shriek as I try to stop the rivers advancing in all directions across lesson plans, student work, and borrowed books. I eat my salad while I read student writing and end up dropping little ranch-dressing-soaked bits into my lap. I've always wanted to be the oh-so-professional, polished teacher, but instead I'm the spit-wash queen, constantly repairing the front of my jacket after lunch.

My students fill my head from September to June and there doesn't seem to be much room for anything else. How do I stop thinking about them and concentrate on that Jeep that just slowed down in front of me before I roll my new Mini Cooper into its bumper and break my headlight? I wish I knew.

You can bet my husband wishes I could figure it out.

I'll admit it, I guess. I don't seem to pay attention. I'm clumsy and absentminded, but I do know this: just like in my first-grade experience years ago, students are the first to offer a hand up. When I slide through the soda spill at the front of the room they may be sniggering, but they pick up the papers flung in all directions and ignore my flaming face. Teaching has taught me about the essential goodness in people—in teenagers, even—the wish to help, not hurt. Grace comes in odd ways: the fire drill just when I needed a break; the parent who stops me in the cereal aisle to say how much she appreciates my work on a day when my overheads jammed in the copy machine, my pay check got lost en route from the district office, and no one laughed at my jokes. (In fact, my student Molly told me they were stupid!) Sometimes it is just the grace of a good night's sleep because I know I've done all I can for kids who need it. I'd like to be elegant, but I can settle for being effective, because that's the work that leaves a mark.

stopping at a lunchroom table

Everything, even darkness and silence, has its wonders.
—HELEN KELLER

I don't know why I stopped. I just noticed these three boys spread far apart at a table, last lunch of the day. One was spearing noodles in a runny red sauce; one was chewing a sub sandwich with a deliberate concentration, as if avoiding all eyes; one had finished eating and just stared ahead, chin resting on his backpack. I knew they were deeply alone. I sat down beside the one I recognized and said, "Hey, Sean."

"Hi, Mrs. Kittle," he said. He tucked his chin into his polar fleece jacket and peeked a glance at me, then looked away.

"So, how are you?"

He rooted around in his backpack. He pulled out a spiral notebook open to a page filled with drawings before he answered, "I'm good." He ducked into his collar again, studying his notebook, pen in hand.

I turned to the student across from me. "Hi, I'm Mrs. Kittle."

I caught him mid-chew. "I'm Kevin," he managed.

"Are you a sophomore?" He shook his head.

"I'm a junior." He paused. "And this is my first day."

"No kidding. Well, welcome to Kennett," I smiled. I introduced him to Sean, asked about his classes, gave him directions to his next one, and tossed my napkin in my empty bowl. Time to move on.

I took a last look at Sean's book. "Hey, what do you have there?"

And out it came. There was a category of food items: Doritos, eggs, canned soups, apples, cereal. A drawing of a large rectangular space: clothing and books on one side; toys in bins, and blankets in boxes on the other. Two sizes of blankets: adults and children. There were small, pudgy drawings of people lined up at the door, some to help and some to shop, all wearing small smiles. My hand slowed as I turned pages of lists: what to buy and who had the best prices in town; the current prices of a dozen or more RVs; the careful catalog of best-loved toys, from SpongeBob to Superman; and then a floor plan with a place to relax and play games. I looked up, puzzled.

He explained, "It's Sean's Magical Book Mobile Dream Shop. See?" He pulled an Auto Trader magazine from his backpack and turned to a marked page. "This is the one I want." The used RV was $33,500. "This one is perfect. I'll outfit it just like this," he flipped back to the first page, with the floor-plan map, "and I'll drive around and deliver supplies to the homeless. It's my dream."

I walked back to my room deep in thought. It had felt like the usual lunch: my bland soup looking a little desperate in its Styrofoam cup; the smiling lunch ladies; haggard administrators; pizza and pretzels and frosted minidonuts wrapped in cellophane. And then I thought of those golden tickets in *Willy Wonka and the Chocolate Factory*. Everyone's searching madly for them, looking in case after case of chocolate bars, but only a few bars had a real golden ticket hidden inside.

And I felt like I'd just found one.

The students streamed by me in the halls as I went on to class.

I bet there's one.

And another.

And another.

I entered my room determined to tug a little and find out what's inside those other wrappers.

Josh

Nothing you do for children is ever wasted.
They seem not to notice us, hovering, avoiding our eyes,
and they seldom offer thanks,
but what we do for them is never wasted.

—GARRISON KEILLOR

There was a sweet little redhead in my seventh-grade class whose mom called to ask if I'd talk to him about alcoholism. The call was awkward, and I think only now about how hard it must have been for her to call me. I was one of the seven teachers Josh saw every day. Mom and I had never met. Parents watch their children close the doors on elementary school and begin adolescence, and both children and territory are suddenly unfamiliar. I imagine she felt she had nowhere to turn.

She called me because Josh mentioned a poem I'd written. I knew immediately what she meant. I'd shared it with my class reluctantly; not only was poetry a mysterious genre to me, but the content was a risk. Poems capture moments in time, one image, and I had one: waiting for the bus on a windy, cold day, late to school, feeling ill, wanting desperately to stay home. I could see my mom at the front window watching me, and I wanted to race up the stairs to our

33

house. I stood sniffling, knowing I had to leave so she could care for my dad. He was drinking again.

Most students said little or nothing after I read. Jeremy finally cleared his throat and said, "That was depressing. Write about something funny next time," and I grimaced rather than say what I was thinking.

But Josh heard my story and knew. He had gone home and said something about it to his mother and she needed my help. Maybe he would talk to me if I tried. He needed to talk to someone, she said. As I listened to her plea I thought about Josh. He and I barely spoke; I didn't feel close enough to him to speak of something so private. I had 150 seventh graders to teach every day. I couldn't remember any conversations with Josh that I'd had that would allow for this one, but Mom was insistent, pleading, and I agreed to try.

After class at my desk, Josh pulled a seat near mine. He seemed excited to have this personal time with me. He was animated; his eyes bright, he tipped up the brim on his baseball hat and grinned, freckles spilling like stars across his cheeks. He snickered over a knock-knock joke.

I almost lost my nerve. "So, Josh, um, your mom called me."

He stiffened. An invisible shield went up between us. Instantly his eyes were guarded and all the brightness was a memory. It was a distinct imprint, though, that moment when his guard was down. I wished I knew him better.

I continued, "She said you mentioned my poem, and she thought you might want to talk to me about your dad's drinking." There, I'd said it.

I watched color rise up his throat and across his cheeks as he sat back in his chair, lowering his eyes. "No," he said, and then, "No," again. He even started to stand, then slumped, "I'm fine—"

"I'm sorry," I said, fumbling with the wire spiral edge of my plan book.

He stayed silent, pressed back against his chair, feet curled beneath him.

I gave him a few more moments and offered something stiff like, "Well, if you do need to talk," before I signed his pass back to math class. We never spoke of it again.

Not all kids want to share life stories. Not all will write of their struggles to understand the complexities at home. Josh wrote about baseball every time he could; he was hiding. But he had a teacher who took on the terror of alcoholism and wrote about it. I like to think that helped him do his own healing once he was ready.

This world of teaching is thorny, knotty, dense, and unpredictable. It's the only thing I know for sure.

Lucas

The challenge of helping children write well—and live well—
is bigger than any of us and bigger than any of our theories.
It's a challenge that's big enough to live for.

—LUCY CALKINS

*H*e filed into class on the first day of school with all of the others. He would have been easy to miss, hanging just at the edge of the boy in front of him, silently placing his backpack on the rack and taking his seat with my other fifth graders. He did everything I asked him to do that day and all of those after.

Every single day except one.

Lucas smiled shyly from behind a smooth line of bangs that hung across his eyebrows. But those smiles were rare. Most often I remember his serious pale blue eyes watching me, sometimes looking right through me to something on the blackboard or beyond. He was small framed and oh, so quiet. Lucas was the child who shrinks at his desk, taking up very little space in the room. Some days I didn't really notice him at all. The other kids liked Lucas, but it didn't seem to matter a whole lot. It didn't change his somber look.

He played ball at recess; he wrote dutifully in his journal. Lucas was breathing, but he wasn't living. I know it now, but I didn't think it through at the time. I was remembering to buy snacks at the grocery for my many students who came to school hungry. I was filling out forms on Carl, so far behind his classmates that I was afraid to promote him to middle school. I was designing units for a grade level I'd never taught. I was a new mother and a graduate student and Lucas was joyless, but obedient. He was one of the last things on my mind.

I remember peppering him with questions when I found out he was from New England. "Wow, it must be so different there," I said.

"Yeah," he replied. Nothing more. I stopped myself from asking, "Do you miss it?" because I knew he must. I didn't want him to feel sad. He had left behind a lifetime of friends; it had to hurt.

His father was the new pastor at the church by the lake and his mother was in front of school to pick him up every day after school. They all liked their new home; he had several younger siblings. It seemed so simple. His mom checked with me to see if Lucas was adjusting all right, her eyebrows forming a sharp *V* in the center of her forehead. Lucas completed all of his homework and answered quickly when called on in class. We both walked away from our fall parent conference feeling mostly satisfied.

In late November my students were writing furiously, their stories filling class books and file trays; our writing workshop was humming. Lucas began a piece about ice skating on the playground at recess. I was fascinated.

"You skate right across the basketball courts?" I asked, my eyes wide in surprise. "No way, really?"

"Yes, we do! All winter long! Every single day," he answered, with an intensity in his look and voice that I couldn't miss. It was Lucas come alive; I suddenly saw what had been missing.

"Tell me more, please. I've never seen that," I said seriously, stunned by the child unfolding before me. He was suddenly not so fragile.

"When the hills around the school get a new snow it is like frosting. We have to shovel off the new snow so we can skate, but it doesn't take long and we race with our shovels." Lucas had his fists clenched holding the shovel in his memory as he told me. His cheeks flushed as he continued, "I used to pass out the shovels. I could put my skates on the fastest, so I got to pass out the shovels and all of the kids would line up by the door and wait for *me*."

He stopped and looked out the window to the blacktop wet with rain. I heard a hiccup noise as he looked away from me, but I knew instantly it was a sob. He was shaking. "When is this rain going to stop?" he shouted suddenly, his rage a thunder in our room. Lucas leapt up and was standing at the window, his fist raised, daring it to continue. I was afraid he was going to put his small hand right through the window. We were all frightened into silence.

The answer, of course, was that it would rain until April sometime; that's winter in the Northwest, but I wasn't about to tell Lucas. I put my arm around him and took him out of the room, signaling the teacher next door to cover for me. Lucas and I found a corner in the library and talked about Massachusetts and ice skating and the frigid cold of below-zero weather. We talked about missing friends and being new and having every little thing in your life change suddenly, irrevocably, feeling powerless and small. Lucas stepped into a deep depression that afternoon that lasted until spring, but at least he was living again, and we were able to help him. By May he played baseball and hollered with the other kids at recess.

Franz Kafka said, "Reading ought to be an axe to break up the frozen sea within us." Yes, and so should writing. We teach kids to write so that the stories lying secret in their hearts may find a voice. They may wrestle with uncertainty, fight the bad guys, or turn to smile as the crowd cheers their winning goal, all with a chewed-on pencil and a simple sheet of paper. The teaching of writing is the teaching of living, and it must be done well: for Lucas and for all of them.

our last day of school

Life has to be lived, that's all there is to it.
—ELEANOR ROOSEVELT

I crawled out of my car on the last day of school one year into the arms of my husband, who was playing with our dog in the driveway. I sobbed for several minutes before I could even speak. "Darlene," came out in hiccups and snorts, and he held me close, kissing my hair and stroking my back with his strong hands. He was impatient to hear my story, but he waited mutely until I could tell him. I felt like a mess, all snotty nosed and uncomposed.

In one hand I held her letter still creased in even rectangles where she'd folded it tightly before handing it to me. In my other hand car keys still warm from the ignition dug into my fist painfully, but not painfully enough. We sat on the steps of our rented house and I stroked Smedley's golden fur as I read my husband the letter Darlene had given me on this, our last day together. She'd written it in detention. While my class played softball and enjoyed a family BBQ, Darlene had been trapped in the resource room, not allowed to participate. The classroom aide told me she'd written almost the entire afternoon. She'd never complained about her punishment, she'd simply asked for paper to write to me.

I replayed our meeting that morning, the two of us facing each other across the barrenness of my room stripped of student work and life, prepared for the silence of summer. Darlene's stoicism met my anger. She didn't know why she'd stolen all of our pentominoes, used to solve spatial problems in math, and kept them hidden under her bed until her father saw them and returned them to school that morning. My principal had been angry when I had admitted I hadn't noticed that they were missing; sure, I was a new teacher, but I needed to be a better steward of school property. I agreed. I was mortified; Darlene would hear from me. I returned to my classroom embarrassed and defeated.

I believe it was Chrissy who brought me the empty egg carton as I walked to the front of the room, asking why I had taken out all of the coins from our "Race with Real Money" game. For two years that game had remained a testimony to my trust in kids. Not a penny had ever come up missing, although my colleagues had rolled their eyes at my naïveté. I had stocked the game with more than ten dollars of my own money so my students could practice making change when finished with other math work. They were required to count and organize the money before they returned the game to the shelf, and every time it was perfectly intact. Until today. Only a few pennies remained in one cup; the quarters, dimes, and nickels had vanished. Even the fifty-cent pieces I'd made a special trip to the bank to get were missing. I was crushed. I knew it was Darlene and my rage felt all-consuming. What else was missing?

I don't remember my words or the lessons that lugged us toward recess, but when the others rose to leave I ordered Darlene to stay in her seat. The students scurried for coats, casting looks at each of us as they went out the door. I arranged good-bye presents on my desk, struggling for words. I knew Darlene's history and I wanted to control my temper. But I'd always been nice to her, compassionate and careful. Why had she done this to me?

Since she couldn't explain the pentominoes, I moved to the coins from our game. "Did you take the money?" I asked firmly, a don't-mess-with-me voice that insisted on the truth.

"Yes," her voice trembled in reply.

"How could you betray me like that?" I asked. "I trusted you. You have broken trust with the entire class, Darlene. How long has this been going on?"

"I took the pentominoes in February," she answered.

"What?" I spit the word at her. "How could you?"

She stood before me like a small shield struggling to deflect a barrage of arrows. She knew she couldn't win, but she would bear it. I could see the girl who had somehow endured the sexual abuse of her father for years, and never said a word. It was her older sister who filled us in; they were all victims. Social services had intervened, but tried to keep the kids together. Since no one wanted four adolescents, the girls remained at home. The father promised to leave them alone, but nothing had changed. We were sure of that.

I was trapped here in this room with her; my anger was wrong, yet I couldn't get it under control. Darlene had embarrassed me in front of the staff of our small elementary school; my older colleagues were surely tsk-tsking me at this very moment. Dammit, her life was not my fault, and I could not look the other way after she had stolen so many things. I was sure to uncover more as I packed boxes for the summer. I couldn't suspend her or, God forbid, send her home. I told her she would have to serve detention in the resource room for the rest of the day. Field day was a privilege she would forgo to pay for what she'd done. I felt guilty taking anything from her, but she seemed relieved. I believe she thought I would hit her or brutalize her with more than just words. Certainly she had a right to expect savagery from adults.

I tried to enjoy our sunny afternoon. It had been a wonderful year, and one parent after another came up to thank me for my work. But I felt Darlene's absence and regretted my words to her. It was our last day, after all. Where was my compassion? Spent, perhaps—by June there isn't much left to give.

When we returned to the room, to empty desks, Darlene was there waiting. I smiled at her and she offered a small, shamed look. "Do you need a bag for your things?" I asked, wanting to give her something.

"No thanks," she said, watching my eyes for forgiveness, I believe.

"It's okay, Darlene," I whispered finally, "I know you didn't mean to." I couldn't bring myself to say "Have a nice summer." I couldn't think what months at her house would hold.

She breathed deeply and reached out with the note. "Here, Mrs. Kittle, I'm sorry I didn't bring you a present."

I don't need a present, Darlene. It was a pleasure to be your teacher were words that didn't come to me. Instead I said nothing, fighting tears as I wrapped her in a hug and winced when she squeezed me too tightly.

The buses had departed before I unfolded her note. It was thick, several pages of her fat script in pencil. Her apology was sincere, her explanations a jumbled mess of things she herself did not understand. She just couldn't control herself no matter how she tried. And then she asked if I'd let her come and live with me. She begged. She said she knew I'd say no, but she'd never wanted anything as much as this and couldn't I please just let her live at my house and be her mother? She promised to be good and my sobs absorbed her pleas for forgiveness and mercy. Mercy that I knew I wouldn't offer. I was newly married, twenty-three years old, and just learning how to manage my own life. I couldn't mother such a broken child. Of course I couldn't. But how could I say no, knowing what I was leaving her to?

It was an early lesson in what this work as a teacher would require. I would know too much about things I didn't want to understand. I would be unable to alter the madness that rules in too many homes. And I would return each fall. At least in the six hours each day when children come to the safety of school I can be kind.

Perhaps in that one lesson they will find a vision of another way to be.

second chance

*Life's lessons aren't simply for us,
they're for the lives that will come.*

—CHRIS CRUTCHER

*T*he usual noise accompanied my class into the room like a churning cloud of dust in the desert just as a storm begins. Shouts, giggles, and sarcasm swirled around my seventh graders, with their notebooks held tightly to their chests, shirts untucked, and hair recently combed, as they made a calculated, but casually cool entrance to English class. They were trying hard not to appear to be trying hard twelve-year-olds. I smiled.

I fielded stories and excuses and fumbled for my grade book to record attendance. Thirty bodies entered in rapid succession while twenty-eight others exited. It was a small door. I watched the sideways glances and shy looks as boys and girls brushed against each other, giggling in unison.

Crystal had long, wavy brown hair with a hint of red that glowed under fluorescent lights. She was chubby and awkward in jeans and a large sweatshirt, and she entered with Susan fixed to her side. Susan seemed to be escorting her in a maternal way, I noticed with amusement. Although puzzled, I couldn't linger on it. I had absence slips to sign, stories to listen to, journals to return, and then the bell rang suddenly, signaling it was time for the show.

I turned toward the chalkboard and noticed Crystal sitting at the extra teacher's desk facing the class. Crystal wasn't confrontational, so I was curious, but also a little annoyed. Class never seemed to start promptly, and I had things to do. I could, of course, have just barked at her to take her seat, like a command general at the front line, a strategy promoted by several of my colleagues, but it wasn't my way. I approached quickly. Crystal had pushed the chair away from the desk and was reclined against the back, legs outstretched before her. The rest of my students kept talking, ignoring us. Susan had been watching me, and as I drew near she bolted to Crystal's side.

I said, "Crystal, what's up?"

"Mrs. Kittle," Susan whispered urgently, "Crystal can't sit at a student desk today."

I turned to Crystal, wondering if they were playing a trick on me. "Crystal, why are you sitting here?" I asked with a grin.

She stared at the desk and spoke quietly. "My legs hurt."

I kneeled beside her. I was trying to be considerate, but I was feeling rushed. I said quietly, "What's the matter, Crystal?"

She turned to look at me, resignation in her dark blue eyes almost shielded by a wall of hair. "My dad hit me," she spoke clearly, then looked away as she continued. "He beat me so badly last night I just can't move my legs into those little desks. Mrs. Kittle," she glanced up as she said my name, "please let me sit here."

I was flooded with rage as I swallowed. My stomach turned and my hands were shaking. I answered quickly, "Of course you may sit here." I rose to my feet and paused to recover my equilibrium.

I turned to begin class. There were thirty kids waiting. I was determined to follow my plan. Somehow. My thoughts never left Crystal and I worked hard to glance at her only as often as I addressed the other students. Once I stopped midsentence and began to think about her, but I recovered. Parallel thoughts raced along in my head: paragraphs and child abuse. Teaching and protecting. Sentence structure and the sound of a fist or a belt hitting her pale legs. Checking for understanding beside the real test I faced as a teacher. I hadn't studied for this. The clock moved toward the end of the hour.

I assigned homework and moved toward her.

"Crystal, sweetheart, I can help you. I can't let you leave at the end of class," I spoke in a near whisper and ignored the questions coming from others. "Please stay here, Crystal. We need to talk."

She tensed, but stayed silent.

"Mrs. Kittle, I don't have my book," a student called.

"You can borrow mine," I answered, cutting him off.

"What page?"

"It's on the board. All of you, the assignment is on the board. Please record it before the bell." I was interrupted by the solid tone coming from the hall.

"Thanks for all the time to copy down the assignment, Mrs. Kittle. Now I'll be late to math." Jared glared as he spoke.

"You'll make it," I sighed and turned again to Crystal.

I'd been handed a second chance to fix the mistakes I'd made three years ago with Angie, and I was afraid. I hadn't thought how this might happen again; I had pretended it wouldn't. I still didn't know what to do, but I had to do better than last time. I hovered by the front desk, subtly trying to block her exit. She sat unmoved.

Susan hesitated to leave. "It's okay," I said, "I'll take care of her." Susan lingered by her desk, her long, thin legs wrapped in jeans, her arms crossed before her, fingernails digging into her sides as my room emptied. "Thank you for helping, Susan. You're a good friend," I said. "Go ahead and go to your next class."

"Bye, Crystal," she said, "call me." The halls simmered and slowly grew silent as I pulled up a chair next to Crystal's side.

I remembered the same scrape of metal leg against linoleum years ago in my fifth-grade classroom as I dragged a chair next to Angie's desk, her journal in my left hand. Her large, blue eyes were wide, her skin pale and almost blue beneath the shocking black hair she wore trimmed close to her head and above her ears. Angie was fragile and ghostlike, staring hard at her journal as she ran her fingers back and forth across the pencil on her desk. It was lunchtime. I'd read the class journals while eating leftover pasta at my desk. Angie's words had been written and erased, but the remaining shadow was clear and it took little effort to see the story of being raped by her fourteen-year-old neighbor when she was in kindergarten. I had read and reread and wondered what to do. She had wanted me to know, and she hadn't. I was going to have to betray her confidence; I felt it with sickening clarity. It was only the second week of school and we'd talked about journals, but I'd encouraged them to write honestly, promising their words would stay between us.

I'd forgotten one might write something like this. I imagined complaints about siblings or sad stories of sick pets: ten-year-old things. I hadn't said that some words would have to be repeated. It is the law and I should have warned her. I knew better; I'd just forgotten. I'd brought her in from recess hoping somehow the words would come.

"Angie," I began, "I read your journal—"

"I erased that," she interrupted.

"Yes, but I could still read it. Angie, I'm sorry. I should have told you I would have to tell about something like this." She tensed, then glanced at the door and moved slightly away from me. She was going to run. She opened her mouth to speak and the tears started down her left cheek in a steady stream. She looked away.

"Angie, I talked to Mrs. Franke and—"

"You said you wouldn't tell!" Her anguished voice stunned me.

"I know. I was wrong." I felt tears on my cheeks; I saw Angie's frightened eyes. "I forgot that there are things that teachers *have* to tell."

Mrs. Franke appeared at the door. "Angie," she said, "can we please talk?"

"No. Mrs. Franke, it was a lie. It was pretend," Angie spoke rapidly.

Mrs. Franke shook her head and looked at me. "Why don't I come back later?"

I nodded, but I didn't want to be alone. I was the worst kind of teacher. We sat in silence for the next several minutes until the voices of kids began outside our door. I rose and walked to my desk; Angie dug her pen into the cover of her notebook. From this moment of personal failure I had to recover and begin my afternoon lessons. I had no confidence; I didn't know what to say to my students anymore.

It was midway through math when a policeman appeared at our classroom door. My god, in uniform even; this was criminal. I saw Mrs. Franke beside him through the glass pane and quickly looked at Angie. Her eyes darted from her desk to the door as it opened.

The policeman smiled and motioned for her to join him in the hall. I wasn't surprised she wouldn't look at me as she left. My students barely contained their curiosity and I sighed at all the wreckage I'd created by being careless. My head pounded.

I taught the rest of the day as a robot. I worked through our agenda, but I was a shell of the teacher I was in the morning. I learned later that Angie denied the events and tearfully begged them to believe her, but the police officer investigated and the boy not only admitted it; he gloried in having it known. I knew it was true; I could see it in her eyes when I showed her the journal. But telling doesn't always make things better. Angie's mother was furious at the school's interference; these neighbors were lifelong friends. She refused to press charges; she believed Angie contributed to the "misunderstanding" years ago.

Angie endured my teaching for the rest of the year. She never forgave me; I didn't forgive myself. When I heard she was locked up as a fifteen-year-old for stealing morphine from a dying cancer patient, I felt some complicity—for being incapable of helping her when the chance came to me.

"Crystal," I said tenderly, "your father should not beat you; it isn't okay." I wanted to wrap her in my arms, but I kept my distance.

She nodded; her face was serious, tears absent.

"I have to tell Mr. Johnson so we can help you." I knew this next step, at least. "You know Mr. Johnson, don't you?" I asked as I rubbed her forearm with my hand.

"Yes."

"Let's go and talk to him, okay? We need to figure out what to do." I took her hand. She gripped the side of the desk and rose without bending her knees, squeezing my hand tightly. I put my arm around her. "Crystal, I'm so sorry," I said to her beautiful auburn hair.

I only had a minute to talk to the counselor, but he surmised the situation quickly and took control. He had done this so many times before. I had to get back to my classroom. The police sent Child Services to pick Crystal up at school before the end of the day. Her father arrived for her at 2:30. Mr. Johnson filled him in. I remember the angry shouts echoing down the empty halls that afternoon. My heart beat furiously.

Crystal was placed in temporary foster care and it was almost the end of the school year before I saw her again. She said little; it was awkward when we met. We both wished I didn't know her story.

L̲ast night as I walked the neighborhood with my husband and our dog, my mind traveled freely as I breathed in the cooling air of nightfall and the melting snow around us. I suddenly saw Crystal's face, and then Angie's—the two are forever connected in my memory. I tried to create a safe haven in my room: a small release from their everyday confusion and fear. We read great stories, and maybe for a little while they lived a different life. I wondered aloud what had become of them in the fifteen years and thousands of miles that now separate us. My husband listened, then wrapped me in a hug. I stared at a black sky filled with patterns of stars, the same stars that lit their night, wherever they are.

just when I thought
I knew everything

*One of teaching's great rewards is the daily
chance it gives us to get back on the dance floor.*

—PARKER PALMER

Colleen was a typical eighth grader in many ways: not quite confident; on the edge; happy and buoyant one day; terribly sad the next. Her writing was genuine and she seemed to care about her schoolwork, but she just couldn't get it in on time. No surprise. School takes a backseat at this age, but I was weary of excuses and apologies when she approached me at the beginning of class one Monday. A group of students stood before me with questions and books to return, I heard loud voices from the hall that I really should have stepped out and checked on, because the bells weren't working and everyone seemed to be taking advantage, arriving to class several minutes late. And here was Colleen. It was fourth period and I was tired from the weekend, frazzled and impatient. Colleen began to tell me she didn't have her homework. Homework was due every Monday; after four months, I didn't want to hear her excuses anymore.

"Fine, you don't have it. It isn't like this is the first time. You'll just have to take a late work grade." I turned to grab my grade book and a pen to take attendance. She walked to her seat angry. She fixed me with a glare as I started class. I knew I was being short, but I had covered the ground patiently with her many times.

Class started and I explained a school district writing prompt they needed to complete. It was simple: tell about an important person in your life, why they were important, and so on. Colleen got out paper and began like everyone else. I returned to my desk and looked at the homework journals. I glanced up frequently to see if students needed help, but I was often lost in their writing. Correcting journals is a pleasure, as students are free to write what they want. The next time I swept the room with my eyes I stopped on Colleen, who was hunched over her paper, crying.

Yes, I felt guilty. I figured my short temper had nailed her on a bad day and I rose to apologize. As I approached her desk the disintegrating tissue in her left hand told me she had been crying for awhile.

I kneeled down beside her and whispered, "What's the matter?"

She tried to glare at me through her tears but quickly dropped her eyes and reached for the box of tissues I held out to her.

"Are you having trouble with the writing?" She shook her head quickly. "Do you want to talk outside?" Again, a quick shake of her thick brown hair. She struggled for words, took a deep breath, and started.

"My mom is in the hospital and I don't know if she is going to be okay. She's my important person," she sobbed, "and I can't write about her today."

"Don't worry—"

She interrupted, "That's what I was trying to tell you. I spent the whole night at the hospital. My mom had a heart attack. That's why I don't have my journal," she spat the last word at me.

This is a humbling job.

We think we know everything sometimes.

We barely know the beginning.

Lauren

You don't have to suffer to be a poet;
adolescence is enough suffering for anyone.

—JOHN CIARDI

She was hunched over a computer station in our writing lab at 7:10 in the morning. She'd come for help on her admissions essay, a senior with a deadline creeping nearer like a shadow, threatening to swallow her. Three other students worked silently in the lab and the opening was there for Lauren. Our eyes met. I said, "So, how can I help?"

She pushed off against the desk and came sliding toward me on her rolling chair. She had her writing portfolio in her lap and she started in about grading and her two essays and frustration and being a bad writer. Finally she said, "I just have no confidence."

"In this piece?" I asked, looking at the teacher comments in orange across the page.

"In anything. In me. I'm sorry; I'm going to start crying," she answered, and her brown eyes were full as she quickly turned away. The halls just beyond our classroom door were entirely empty, their silence hollow around us.

"I don't know how to write," she continued, "my SATs were bad"—she swallowed the start of tears again—"I can't write this essay."

"Can I see what you've done?"

She gave me her notebook and began telling me about the two pieces. One told of her experience volunteering at a summer camp for terminally ill children. The other told of a surprise party her friends threw for her when they knew she was feeling down. Both had glimpses of great writing, a few lines that worked well, but the over-all effect was flat. She compared the grades. "This one I worked really hard on and got a 73, and this one I barely worked on and I got an 88. The grades make no sense to me." Trust me, I wanted to say, grades don't make sense even to most writing teachers. If we could abandon them we would. Writers need feedback, not evaluation.

"Well, let's forget about grades while working on this," I said, "because we just need to focus on telling one of these stories well for your admissions essay. Tell me more about Camp Sunshine."

As Lauren talked, I wrote down what she said. One line after another, a natural story began to unfold. Lauren could tell about this experience well, but she cramped up when writing of it. This was a kid who needed to write more, but her teacher's evaluation had cranked up the pressure on every line. This pressure had turned off the faucet of free thinking. It was almost rusted shut. A little drip escaped now and then, but not the flow she needed to write her story.

I continued to ask questions about the experience she had at camp. I used lines from her original piece to help. "You say you walked around the other counselors in circles; what does that mean?"

"I was really nervous. I didn't know how I was supposed to act around these kids. It was the first day and no one had told me what to do."

"That's a great line to show that. I felt your confusion when I read it. What we need is more information like you just told me so the reader is there with you as the students get off the buses at camp, and they'll be walking in circles with you because they don't know what to do either."

Lauren told me the details and I wrote them down. Lauren laughed as she talked about the girl who had the biggest impact on her. As she listed phrases and moments, this girl, Janie, began to find a shape.

I blocked out a writing piece with Lauren hovering near my elbow. I was careful to say, "This is one possibility for this piece," so Lauren retained control over how to write the story. "I'm not sure this will work, but if you put the details about Janie in your story, and you show all of these things you tried to tell us at the start, the reader will get it. The reader will know why this camp experience mattered to you because they will be there with you and it will matter to them."

Lauren nodded and looked at my notes. She smiled. "I feel so much better. I was dreading this, but now I feel good about this." I sent her off to work on the piece and we made a date to meet the following Thursday during writing lab.

Now if I had to place a bet, I'd say that the writing is not going to go easily for her. I'm not going to pretend that our fifteen minutes together changed her. And I'm not going to say that at the end of our work on this essay, even if it is fabulous and gets her into a college she wants to attend, she will have the confidence in herself that she knows is missing. But I do know two things.

Lauren needed unhurried time to talk about what she was trying to say in her piece to even have a chance with it. It is the essential prewriting for this writer in this moment. That talk was unlikely to happen in her crowded classroom with the inherent management challenges her teacher faces every day. If twenty kids had come to my writing lab that morning, it might not have happened then, even. But that individual attention is the only thing that will work for writers at times. And I make time as often as I can for my students because real growth happens when I do, and I need to see it. Ninety minutes speed by in my room and I wonder if anyone learned anything some days, but one-on-one with a student, I'm sure. There is an understanding.

And the other thing I know is writing can overcome all kinds of fears and unhealthy relationships. I open that door. The student walks through. I stand on one side and wave as a student goes on without me, often without looking back. And I am deeply satisfied.

no evidence of achievement

Tests serve a very specific purpose: to weed out,
to scatter everyone along that elegant and
immoral slope we call the bell curve.

—JIM BURKE

I'm sitting beside Russell, who can't write about "the most important person in his life," even if it is the topic of the standardized achievement test, because there really is no one. I've suggested every person I can think of and they have all abandoned him. At fourteen, Russell's never known his father. His mother works three jobs and hasn't had a meal with him in months. His brother has moved out of the house and doesn't visit. Russell has a television, but he doesn't own a bicycle. In fact, he told me he can't ride one. His house sits at the end of a gravel road far from town. He has never played on a sports team. I believe in the seven months he's come to school, I have never seen him smile.

Russell came to kindergarten not reading. The only color he could identify in September was "chocolate." He had never been read to at home. Most of the other students in his class had books of their own; a parent, sibling, or grandparent who loved to read; and some knowledge of the alphabet letters and sounds that create words. Russell had a long way to go before he even began in school. When he came to me nine years later, he held a book at a far distance from his face and squinted painfully at the page, forcing out word after word. Of course he needed glasses and the school would provide them—had, in fact, but he refused to wear them. Russell had one thing he was proud of: he was a tough guy. Tough guys don't wear glasses.

So on testing day, Russell and I are at a standoff. He isn't playing around here; he can't even pretend with this writing topic. I finally quit pretending he should be able to. After whispering encouragement for several minutes, I left him alone.

He didn't write a word.

M y colleague told me about a second grader in her classroom this year. The girl is the strongest writer in the room. She's inquisitive and bright, has a varied vocabulary, and writes with a command of language gleaned from her love of reading. When the teacher gave out the district writing test in the spring, this girl listened attentively to the instructions. Silence began. She stared hard at her paper without moving her pencil. Tests have strict conditions and teachers are told not to intervene or coach students, so that the writing sample will reflect only the student's ability. This makes sense most of the time. This teacher couldn't understand what was happening and finally stopped by the girl's desk after ten minutes to say, "Are you okay? Do you understand what to do?"

She said, "Yes."

When the testing period ended that day the paper was entirely blank. The next day students were given their papers back and asked to reread what they had written and finish the story. Again this little one wrote nothing.

The writing prompt seemed simple enough: "Write about one thing you'd like to ask your parents to do with you this summer." Once the test was over the teacher asked the girl why she didn't write anything.

"Mrs. Hughes, I can't ask my parents to do anything this summer. My mom is *really* sick." This child would've had a chance if the topic had been cancer.

These writing samples will certainly earn the lowest score, "no evidence of achievement." Although Russell has written several competent essays for me in class this year, he will fail this test. And although that seven-year-old has exceptional writing skills, the test will mark her as failing. The scores will tell the public that for all the dollars spent on education, we have been unable to teach these kids how to write. And people will believe that. Rather than question whether the test truly measures individual ability or achievement, they'll believe the school and the teachers have failed.

Russell's writing is clear and interesting, if he chooses the topic. Russell has things to say about magic tricks and wrestling. He'll write for a select group of his peers and often for me, but he won't risk failing with someone he doesn't know. He'd rather refuse to do it at all. I've struggled with that. But in northern New Hampshire I've learned that you have to be able to see spring in the brilliant newness of the blue sky, even when surrounded by four-foot snowbanks, just as in my classroom I must be able to see the possibility in this child consumed by hopelessness with walls built around him on all sides. I've had days when he'll let me in, more days when he won't. I could show you his class work and the progress he's making, but these days my opinion isn't valued. We need objective assessment and accountability, our president sputters. If you just leave the assessment to the teachers, children will be left behind.

Not if I can help it.

Consider what we gain by having Russell write his answer and send it off to evaluators paid $9.00 an hour to give it a score. The money could be spent on libraries, lab equipment, and afterschool programs that allow students to follow a passion in art or music or computers. We've squeezed the life out of many of our schools, demanding lower taxes. No field trips, too many children per teacher, few supplies, overburdened administrators, inadequate facilities. Into this volatile mix we add latchkey children begging for attention, love, and respect. We've asked schools to do more with less and then have stood by surprised as floods of teachers walk away and children lose their interest in school. Now we are choosing to spend our money on testing instead of children; I just don't understand.

The true test of my classroom should reside in Russell's portfolio and my colleague's assessment of that little girl. If you'll stop by my room I'll show you writing from each of my students and we can strategize ways to improve it. I'd welcome the help, frankly. But don't believe for a minute that achievement on a test represents who these kids are or what they can accomplish. That would be the real failure here.

Our days are numbered: as teachers, as human beings. Will we waste our time comparing one child to another—pretending that the myriad of life experiences each brings to their desk has no bearing on their performance that day? Will we continue labeling and numbering children to determine where they fall short, even when we know that encouragement and love will move them forward faster and more humanely than this beating with scores and labels and inappropriate expectations?

What will we make of the time given to us?

So much of it all rests in the hands of the teacher.

Katelyn

*If we can embrace, and help our students embrace,
the fact that all writing is just practicing—
practicing to speak what's really in our hearts—
then revision becomes a process of trusting ourselves
to someday write the words we need to write.*

—GEORGIA HEARD

Katelyn burst into the room even on our first day together in her senior year. She moved purposefully past those standing around and took a seat two desks back in the center of the room. She swung her curtain of hair around and put her notebook and pens before her. She met my eyes and gave me a wide, open smile. If you ever hear the phrase "ready to learn," I want you to picture Katelyn. She was eager.

I was busy teaching when someone noticed a large, ugly spider moving across the linoleum near the chalkboard. I turned and said, "Ooo gross," then turned back and kept talking.

Katelyn said, "*Kill it!*"

"No," I said, "the poor thing isn't hurting anyone. . . ." I barely finished. With a hoot a bit like a battle cry, she was out of her seat and smearing it under her black platform shoe before I could stop her.

"Sorry, Mrs. Kittle," she said, smiling. "I *hate* spiders."

Katelyn was indeed a force. But she couldn't write well. She made sure I knew that early on. "Mrs. Kittle, I am a terrible writer. Ask any of my teachers. I suck at it! And I haven't read a book in four years."

You've got to love a challenge in such a lively package.

I started our work as writers with quick writes—those three-minute exercises Linda Rief wrote about. Every day we had three things to write on. It might be Billy Collins poetry and overheads of paintings or news articles or snapshots of my own writing. I've found it helps students find their voices as writers and discover ideas and stories long dormant. I asked the usual at the end of our third quick write one day: "Did anyone find anything important to say?"

Katelyn jumped in, "I did. I didn't write on all three, though. I started writing on the first one and remember you said we could keep going if we found a story? Well, I did." Katelyn fidgeted in her chair, swinging her long hair back and forth behind her, glancing from the words in her notebook to me.

"Do you want to tell us about it?"

She read it over again silently. She looked at me, then said, "Okay." First she told of her senior basketball season that was just beginning and her hope for a winning record, but then her writing shifted to the reason she doesn't really love the sport anymore. She said she looks up in the stands during a game and she used to see her grandfather and father sitting together. Now it is only her grandfather.

I know her father is living, so I asked, "Why doesn't he come anymore?"

"Because of *her.*" Katelyn's eyes widened and flashed at me. The tiger in her appeared. This was a hot subject and probably full of private details, but I continued our public conference because my class learns where to find stories by listening to how their peers find them. But I was apprehensive. Katelyn continued, "He doesn't have time for me ever since *she* came into his life."

There was a muffled "Oooooo" from some of the boys nearby.

Katelyn scowled at them. "She's a—I won't say it. But these guys all know what I'm talking about." She gestured at her friends sitting near. They nodded and chuckled.

"Katelyn, it sounds like a narrative to me," I said. "You have the setting of playing basketball and looking into the stands, but noticing again that your grandfather is sitting alone, to launch your thinking about missing your dad. Then your piece could be about Dad."

"I don't understand," Katelyn replied. She was antsy, pen hovering over her notebook. "What do I write?"

"I'll come help you," I said, then gave instructions to the class so they could begin work without me. Katelyn speaks easily, but the talk doesn't transfer to clear thinking on the page. She seems all bound up when she tries to form her thoughts into sentences. They rub against each other and she gets angry. There are paragraphs that to me obviously need rearranging, but she doesn't see it. She rarely adds enough detail to make her point. I feel we revisit the same lessons with each writing piece, but because she wants to learn, it is easy to keep trying.

We talk about the possible structure of a story about her father. She knows about flashbacks and scenes and we lay those out in her notebook. She's eager to get to work. She tells me the divorce was for the best because both of her parents are happier now, and she likes living with her mother and her mother's boyfriend. But after the divorce her father stopped coming to her basketball games, and he was the one who taught her to play.

"That could be a scene," I say. "Dad showing you how to play basketball. You could structure this differently, with Dad showing you the moves, then being at your games, then not."

Eagerness changes to anxiety. I've just altered the order of what we planned together. It is a natural move for me because I see scenes in a story as movable as chess pieces. Students who have been taught rigid rules about writing balk at this. Katelyn thought we had her draft planned out and now I'm waffling. What I want to teach is that narrative is limitless. Her story could have many structures. What she wants to learn is how to write this piece, start to finish. I sketch a map of what I think she wants to say. She wants all of the roads clearly labeled, so she won't get lost; I want to give her the open road and tell her to find her way. I soon realize it is too soon in her development as a writer. I sketch out the second possibility I spoke of so she has two options to choose from, but I am glancing around at other writers while I talk her through it. I am spending too much time beside her and the corners of the room are starting to unravel.

I want more time with every one of my writers.

Katelyn brings in her first draft the next morning. She wants me to read it before I've even put the agenda on the chalkboard. I skim it quickly while others are arriving so I can tell her something encouraging. "Great start," I say, "I can see the two scenes you've put together."

"What do you mean, 'start'? This is my draft." She is watching my eyes with her wide blue ones.

"Let's talk about it in a minute, okay?" This satisfies her.

Over the next month Katelyn writes nine separate drafts of this story. She has never written as much for anything, she says. Sometimes I can barely tell the difference between her attempts, but at others I can see big leaps of understanding. Draft nine is still choppy and a bit dead, to be truthful. Katelyn is unable to be playful in her writing, and it reads like a hospital chart at times: just the facts. I hear the passion in her voice as she talks about this time in her life, and I want that passion on the page, but she has no idea how to make the transfer. I can't do it for her.

As we work with this piece, the most important thing is that I read and return each attempt right there in class, or I read it at home that night and return it the next day. Katelyn needs regular feedback to grow. We communicate often about the story, so our conferences can be shorthand, cutting straight to where we left off the day before, but still I could spend an hour a day with her if I had the time. There just is never enough time in teaching.

We're starting to pull her story together when she says to me in conference one morning, "This isn't even the *real* story, Mrs. Kittle."

"What do you mean?"

"When my dad threw me out of the house. That was much bigger."

"Hmmmm." I don't think I want to know.

She continues. I hear all of the sad details of her things in garbage bags on the porch and that evil other woman calling to tell her to come and retrieve them. I know this is just one point of view, one side of the story. I know teenagers struggle to see another.

I fumble, "Well, that's a story. Or it could be a scene in your longer piece. It's up to you if you want to write it; it sounds pretty painful." I'm sure this isn't the narrative her father would like her to write, but I also know that telling this story is motivating this writer to learn volumes about writing. It's a story that matters in her life, so she wants to tell it well. That is at the very center of coaching writers: the story that matters.

We no longer need to map out what to write next because she has internalized a structure, which is a plus. I can leave and she'll start working without me.

The next day she has a paragraph about that scene. I wonder if she thinks "paragraph" when I say "scene," because this scene, and most, could be pages of writing. Her piece lacks all of the richness, all of the detail she told me in conference. She is not making the transfer from spoken language to written. She is caught up in what writing is supposed to be instead of telling her story.

I ask her if she'd like to share it with the class and see if they can offer any feedback to help her. She knows the draft isn't what she intended, so she's ready for help. I know she needs another voice to coach her. My students circle desks. By now we've been together through stories of cancer and loss, funny memories of songs we loved most in junior high, Mackenzie's traffic tickets, Carrie's country music, Kyle's constant talking, and Todd's infamous speech to a packed auditorium gathered to discuss the school bond vote. We are family.

When Katelyn finishes reading there is nothing but silence for a few minutes. That respect is essential. I can trust these kids to coach her well. Tom tells her he understands what she's feeling and knows that what she's trying to say is important. I watch him helping her, so earnest in his desire to encourage her, but careful to prompt her for more. Tom knows how to write a painful story and he gives her meaningful suggestions for revision. I'm not sure they've spoken before today, but writing brings connections.

Chet jumps in next. He says, "I went through that with my dad and his new wife; I know what you're talking about." I'm amazed he's awake. I don't think he's been this animated all semester. Chet tells her to draw out the phone call that begins the piece and Katelyn nods in appreciation. She's taking notes on her draft, and I'm on the edge of my seat watching this writing community unfold. I just hope there isn't a fire drill in the next few minutes.

Mackenzie puts her hand up. These girls are not friends; they are seated as far apart as possible. There's ferocious tension between them most days, hot and fiery like coals ready for a cookout. One wrong move and the sneers begin. But today she says, "That's just really great, Katelyn. I think you have something to say that I, for one, would want to read. You could, like, tell some more about the moving out, so the reader can really see it, you know. What did it look like with all your stuff on the porch?"

Katelyn explains. My community of writers is rocking. I've worked all semester for this moment: the sweet harmony of stepping out of the way so students can teach each other. If you had peeked in the window of my classroom, you would have seen my feet dancing under my desk. This is what I'm here for.

Katelyn finished the semester without finishing that piece of writing. It wasn't all the way there when grades closed and final portfolios were due, but when it came time to evaluate her work she marked that essay with a large pink Post-it labeled "taking a writing risk." And what's even better is that risk paid off, in dollars. When Katelyn went to write scholarship essays a few months later, the difference in her writing was obvious. She was not the same student I had met in September. She understood audience and purpose and most of all, how to tell a story. She collected several scholarships at our annual dinner, marching to the front each time with her long, blonde hair swinging and that unmistakable Katelyn grin on her face. She'll be on campus at Plymouth State University in the fall. Can't you just see her?

Maybe I ought to warn them about the spiders.

Emily

A friend told me we spend the majority of our energy
not doing what we most want to do,
not saying what we want to say.
Most energy, she said, serves to keep the lid on.
The soul waits, the heart waits.
But when we write, even a note, we let out soul.

—KIM STAFFORD

A senior girl came to me on an afternoon when deadlines were approaching faster than I wanted, and my spirits were sagging just from the weight of the work to be done. Her kind blue eyes met mine as she peeked over the head of the main office secretary, who asked if I had a minute. I did; a distraction was just what I needed.

She entered my office cautiously, as if she wanted to slip by unnoticed. I was struck by her fine blonde hair, straight and long, and her pretty smile. Small-framed and quiet, she asked if I could take a moment to help her. I expected a complaint of some sort, most likely a course request change, but instead she asked if I would read over her college admissions essay. I was thrilled. A colleague had been sending students to me over the last month. He was drowning in anxious seniors; I was a teacher masquerading as an administrator, too far from a classroom.

I listened as Emily explained that she needed to finish; her application packet was due soon. She had pages of drafting, but she didn't know what to do next. She appeared to have everything together, from her perfect black leather jacket to her remarkable poise, but she had no confidence when she talked about this essay. Her teacher had told her to keep drafting, but she was going nowhere. Anxiety crossed her face like a shadow. I glanced at a handful of pages—tiny print, single-spaced, a formidable read. After a few questions I began.

> I like color. I used to move the furniture around in my room as a child. I like harvest colors of orange and brown and the smell of paint.

I suppressed a sigh. What to say? She wanted a career in interior design; that much was clear. She hadn't a story to carry her essay, though, and I lost hope by the end of page three that we could find one. I doubted I could help; I still remain unsure almost every time I sit with a student to talk about writing. There is much to say, but I fear I'll crush a developing writer with a wrong move. Plus, under this kind of college admissions pressure, few write well. I kept reading, hoping I'd find something to build on. Until there: the last line on page four.

> I had to prepare the room when my mother came home to die.

My word.

"Can you tell me what this means exactly?" I looked up quickly and I'm sure that a crease deepened between my eyebrows.

Emily explained the way she had arranged furniture, used paint and light to create comfort, and designed a space for her mother's needs when the last few months came. I listened. I kept looking at her, so much like my daughter. I wondered how a child moves on after the loss of a parent. She said, "Interior design means creating spaces for living as well as dying," and seemed to pause midthought.

I finally said, "I think that's your story. I know it will be hard to write, but it could really carry this essay."

Several days later she brought me draft two. I eagerly glanced at
the first line.

She was leaving me and all I could do was make it more com-
fortable for her.

I took a slow breath. I told her it was a strong opening line
because of how much it didn't say. Her hand trembled and she
wouldn't meet my eyes. I said that I knew she was careful with her
lead and that its power was stunning. Emily glanced out the window
as grief made a quick journey from her eyes to the lines around her
mouth. She offered me a small smile of thanks. I continued reading.

Growing up in a small town I only had about two friends. I was
very close to my older sister and mother. It was just the three of
us girls; we did everything together. Before our eyes our lives
were changed forever, the worst that could happen was happening. My mom at age 43 was diagnosed with cancer. I couldn't
breathe. Every day I watched her fading away, it was all I could
do. She was the closest person to me in my life and I had to watch
her leave me with the rest of my life in my own hands.
   High school was tough, especially going through it without
friends. I didn't have the time for them. I couldn't be a teenager.
I had to be an adult in order to survive without my mother
around anymore.

I thought of this young girl walking as a ghost in the halls of our
school for four years. Who knew? Her essay told how she gave up
soccer to cook dinners for her stepfather, who couldn't rise from his
grief. Her sister was off to college; her own father was distant. She
saw a path then, she said; one road led to depression and the other
to living. She chose to live.
   I never quite feel prepared to teach the lesson that appears. Emily
needed more than my coaching on structure and mechanics; she
needed to hear how writing might sustain her as a human being. As
I struggled with what to say, she said, "I visited Suffolk this weekend,
and I am inspired to finish this by Friday." She was so vibrant, so

ready to move on. I smiled at her joy; she knew this writing was good and it could carry her forward. I concentrated on editing and sent her on her way.

Another draft came the following week. Her hair was gathered in short pigtails—a few strands fell free across her cheek—and she quickly found a chair and smiled. We were still awkward with each other, and she was anxious not to interrupt my work. I scanned the details of her writing. It was easier to meet her on the page than in that small room with so much I wanted to say, but didn't know how to. She didn't drop the *e* when adding *-ing*, and I noticed, of course, but editing felt so small compared to what she was sharing.

What should I teach her?

Writing is bigger than the details. It can be used for summarizing and persuading, sure, but it can also help you claw your way through a tragedy. Writing releases pain and often brings hope. Meaning is found. Not answers, but strength to continue.

In our small talk Emily mentioned the approaching holiday and her hope for a journal. I found one with pencils for drawing in colors I knew she loved. I wrapped it up and handed it to her at our last meeting. I didn't say all that I was thinking. We were just rest stops on a long road. I wasn't there to give advice. If she found any peace in writing about her mother, it might help her. It seemed like a measly lesson from this aging teacher; I wanted to do more. There just wasn't time.

Months later I passed her in the hall and she smiled. I asked, "Have you heard from Suffolk?"

"Yes! I got in!" She beamed.

And so did I.

honors

a teacher's reeducation

Public education is bountiful, crowded, messy, contradictory, exuberant, tragic, frustrating, and remarkable.

—MIKE ROSE

*I*t isn't quite what you think.

Not quite what I thought.

I resisted teaching honors students for years. *They already get everything,* I'd say. *I need to work with kids who need me.* I've worked in our lowest academic course for juniors—except my class list was half seniors: the ones who'd failed the class the year before. I've spent a lot of time with the middle level—those willing to try, but not too hard—and those trying really hard because they have to. But I'd passed on honors—I'd heard they wear brand-name clothes and challenge their teachers with arrogance and cruelty. Not for me.

And then this year it appeared in my schedule. I didn't say anything at first. I checked the master schedule and saw I could swap it with another teacher if I wanted to, but for me there's always been this karma thing about teaching. I trust to chance. The kids who end up on my class list are there for a reason—our paths collide because they should. So I didn't say anything. I looked at the names and tried not to remember the stories I'd heard about too many of them.

June passed. In July, while I was in class at UNH, I wrote them a letter—a greeting and a nudge about summer reading. But then I never sent it. Who were these kids? I was in honors English at my high school, but I was a complete brat whose only purpose was to torment any teacher who questioned my long absences from class. I hung out with *other* kids, not honors.

Honors seniors?

Yikes.

I kept thinking I knew what *those* kids were like. And yet I knew I didn't. So I said nothing and prepared for the first day of school. I glued their names into my grade book. I started planning. I took their pictures on that first day—one glowing smile after the last—and learned their names.

I couldn't sleep.

I planned more than I could accomplish day after day, looking at the raw matter before me, realizing all it could be. They wrote "I Am What I Am" pieces in the first two days of class and I sat holding them in my hands, staring at the trees that surround my house, wondering what I could teach them; they knew so much already. Two students showed a power and beauty in their writing that scared me a little.

What next?

How?

They already knew.

But that feeling passed. There was plenty they didn't know: like grammar. Good old grammar: I've always called it the retreat of the weak. It's the easy thing to teach—the rules—the symbols—the not-here-but-there—the I-know-and-you-don't independent-appositive-clause-with-a-colon crap that keeps English teachers entertained. I had that. But it wouldn't sustain me. Or them.

I had voice.

Mine.

And a chorus I hadn't tuned into yet.

Because this is what they don't tell you about honors kids: Heidi spent the previous year in Argentina working in an impoverished day care center at a hospital where parasitic worms were pulled from toddlers and children begged for food as she rushed by. She intends to serve others once she finishes a program in international studies. Heidi, who will write and rewrite each piece and then revise once again on her own, is bright-eyed and bright-smiled, eager to know. I want to be the teacher she deserves. She's in honors to absorb every ounce of writing instruction I give her. Her attention is magnetic—a *Star Wars* force field zeroing in on my words and examples—asking questions that make me pause.

Marc makes Chewbacca noises in class and tips his desk sideways over the top of his long legs splayed across the carpet—but he smiles this Ralph-Lauren-Polo-ad-polished grin and apologizes every single time I shush him, so nice I can't help but really like him. His stories have a calculated flow, a rhythm, a completeness. He's the first one with his backpack on hollering good-bye with five minutes left in class, but he writes more than he has to and it sings. He *writes.* He uses what I teach him, so the clicking noises, heavy sighs, and periodic shouts bother me less. And when I didn't know him, when I just saw him with his Army of the Popular in the main lobby, I thought he was Mr. Confidence and I steered clear. Chewbacca is a more accurate nickname.

I thought all there was to Kathleen was the Miss Everything list of all she's done for our school: student body president, Key Club treasurer, cross-country all-star runner and skier, exceptional student. Then I learned she's the maker of homemade birthday cards and cookies for all of her friends. She gives of herself over and over again. She's in tears one day struggling to revise her admissions essay because she puts more pressure on herself than anyone could, and when our letters unit concludes I read her personal letter in my head for days. She steps out and declares her territory as a growing young woman with a fierceness all writers should find. Kathleen taught me more about being a parent of a teenager in one essay than the dozen books I've read over the last ten years. How come these kids are teaching me?

And let me not neglect to introduce you to Taylor: long, dark hair and all-black clothes every day, just returning from a year in France.

He's brilliant, thoughtful, angry. I open his journal one afternoon to read:

> I can't stand this class. I can't believe we are required to write to such ridiculous questions. The only reason I'm even here is because my guidance counselor convinced me it was such a good class. Obviously she never took it.

And I think long and hard about that. By the time they're seniors, students are so sick of the game of school that you have to work harder to sell them on any work at all. Even in an honors course. It's my job. When I hear my colleagues say things like "He doesn't belong in an honors class," I'm afraid I just might toss my coffee in their smug faces. It isn't about what the student brings; it is what the teacher can do for all students in any setting. Taylor's telling me I'm going to need to do more. I'm glad he did. He writes a piece later in the quarter that knocks me out. Brave and unflinching, he dissects religion with a crafty combination of fact and belief. Taylor's voice will be heard; he challenges us to bring all we've got to the table.

I could continue to write, one student after another, one individual story after another, but that still won't begin to capture all they bring to my classroom. There's John, who tried to reset my class clock so we could leave early, except that I caught him. Then he memorialized a football game in a narrative that took us inside the game and inside his soul. Cool writing—finely tuned. There's Sabrina, who's on her way to Calcutta to deliver a check to a charity over the holiday break, funds she raised entirely on her own last summer by organizing a community walk-a-thon. Most people don't know about it because she isn't self-promoting. Her brown eyes are mesmerizing, her laugh a deep-hearted giggle. She's going to make a real difference in the world—absolutely.

And Julie—well, she scared me. She has a self-possession onstage that I admire, and I was sure it would be in all things. She was always in her seat before the start of class with her things ready, waiting in frustration for her peers to get with it. I wanted my class to be a finely oiled machine just for her: orderly, efficient, college-serious, productive. But of course, they all aren't like her, and my classroom isn't perfect any day. Then she writes:

> Oh Johnny Depp, you are so fine,
> I wish so much that you were mine.

And I know she's a regular kid (with very good taste). Later that semester she tells the class, "Okay, I'm going to write about depression and self-mutilation because I think people should understand it," and no one moves. There was a stillness I rarely feel in school: a moment of silent respect, and then Julie's smile, letting us know she's okay, and we all started breathing again. I counted myself lucky to be here in this place with *these* kids trying to craft our voices to say what we really mean. And I counted myself lucky to know this girl in important, complex ways.

Christine is late and she doesn't have a tardy slip and she's writing notes to Pat instead of reading, but she stayed up late one night to draft the story of a little girl losing her father—again and again through losses in her life that always come back to that center—the loss she couldn't right herself from. And she's smart. And sassy. And beautiful. And you'd miss her entirely if you didn't know that story. And I do. I can't believe my luck. I almost chose political science and a life of charming lobbyists instead of coaching writers. Imagine how different my days would be.

I'd have missed Sean, whispering behind his book during silent reading, rarely caught. He's thoughtful and sensitive and smart, and he's come to my office several times for help on his writing, just to make it better. There's Tim, whose brilliance and wit will fillet any teacher caught unawares. Tim's a writer, though—his craft slips in and out of genres with ease. I'd have missed Jay's stories of his exchange in Germany, how he adapted to homestays that weren't welcoming and how he came back stronger, more sure of himself than he'd been just months before. I would have continued to read about Leanne and Tyler and Alex in our local paper: ski races won, trips to Chile and Italy to race the best in the world and beat them. But I would have missed the laughs and the scrambles to continue class work while skiing five or more hours a day, always appreciative of extra help. Leanne is a stitch: funny and original and warm. Tyler is one of the politest young men I know. Alex is mature and real—the kind of girl everyone likes. These students who seem to have everything are considerate and generous; I just didn't expect that.

There's Krista, with her sparkly energy and bubbling laugh, turning in work before it's due, challenging labels and slurs and insensitivity as soon as she hears them, writing passionately about a teacher and friend who is battling cancer. And Liz, who is the first to cheer on her friends, even if they beat her in a ski or road race, because she already knows what is most important in life. Her writing is microscopic, zooming in on the finest detail that illuminates the entire scene. Liz is goodness, kindness, self-control. I wish you knew her.

Matt and Jon start this pounding on the desks these days. It's a rhythm that demands, "lunch de-ten-tion, slap, slap, slap, slap," if a girl is called out for talking. They have started to keep score on the board when I call on kids for disrupting: girls 5, boys 8, to prove each day that I'm sexist. Sure, I'd like to strangle them some mornings, but they are both magnificent writers. Jon has the mind of a poet and has decided to major in writing instead of engineering next fall. Matt will be the engineer, tucked away at St. Michael's College, carefully planning his future, charming every single girl on campus.

Christina and Nicole arrive together, sit at desks side by side, read each other's work and offer smart revisions. Their writing is filled with optimism and determination. They are girls with plans: one will be a hygienist and the other a radio DJ. And then Pat. Where do I start? He calls me Mr. Skittle and rants about kids who watch too much television instead of reading great books. His writing is distinct; it clearly marks territory. He's our next Jack Kerouac; I'm sure of it.

And you might have noticed that this piece is getting long, because one classroom of students is a whirlwind of life and spirit. One person can't be captured in a few lines, and when I try to, I capture only a spark of what I know is a brilliant flame. I say "Molly," and I picture her long, blonde hair wrapped tightly in a bun as she prepares for a dance onstage. She draws you in with blue eyes and a smile and her story of grandparents dying just three months apart after a life together. But then my words are used up and I can't tell you about her giggling-in-trouble-every-other-day-bursting-with-stories self that sits at the back of class. If I do, I'll have no room for Emma, Sarah, Ben, and Sierra. And I can't miss them.

Emma visits most days during her study hall right before class. She's here to swap a book because she powers through novels, college texts, and biographies as fast as I can replace them on my shelves. She's one of the first to challenge a prejudice in class and ask deep questions, while the next minute she's swapping colored marker tattoos with a boy who sits beside her.

Sarah won't say a peep unless you approach her, but you'd better. Then you'll get that dazzling shy smile and her serious writing. She wrote the tightest narrative I've read in years and has no idea how truly talented she is. Perhaps college will show her.

Ben read his fiction piece about street racing in class today. It was the first time I'd heard him read his work, although his voice is a solid presence in everything he writes. Ben uses vocabulary in original, insightful ways and has that essential balance of powerful lines and precise detail that makes words come to life. And he's the one who would hotwire my Mini and park it in the school lobby. He would, but he'd better not.

Sierra arrives in a zebra-print skirt, belted jacket, and wicked-cool shoes. She's the original, the uncompromising president of band and champion of the arts. Sierra lets you know what she thinks no matter how you might flinch. And she won't back down. She knits scarves out of yarn she has dyed with Kool-Aid: brilliant hues of blue and purple and orange. She wants to open a knitting shop some day and I bet she'll play her clarinet as the customers browse.

So it turns out honors is just like every other class I've taught. It's a small room in an ugly plastic portable decorated with Spanish language posters. It's hot—insufferable on warm days—and the wind rattles the floor and ceiling on cold ones. There are too many students—twenty-six in a room built for eighteen—and that's eight extra adult-sized bodies and books and water bottles and jackets and backpacks and senior pictures and best friends and college admissions and formal dances and minor car wrecks and dumped boyfriends and Red Sox Nation, for god's sake. It's adolescence in all its dramatic complexity five days a week—loud and awkward and not yet formed, but eager and willing and ready. It is twenty-six students I won't forget.

Hundreds of stories.

Explosions of laughter.

Moments of deep silence.

All of this. And more.

Kids aren't labels. And I knew that.

I just had to learn it again.

Kleenex® and marriage and learning to teach

Don't reject what readers tell you. Listen to what they say as though it were all true. The way an owl eats a mouse. He takes it all in. He doesn't try to sort out the good parts from the bad. He trusts his organism to make use of what's good and get rid of what isn't. There are various ways in which a reader can be wrong in what he tells you; but still it pays you to accept it all.

—PETER ELBOW

*H*e's reading too slowly and he isn't enjoying it. I watch his hazel eyes move line to line, a puzzled look forming across his brow; he is far too serious for a piece I thought was amusing. He knows I'm watching him and the lines around his eyes show the strain. This doesn't look good. He hesitates to speak when he finishes the final page. He gets up from the couch and begins to wash dishes. It can't be that bad, can it? Say something!

"Well?" I prompt him.

He speaks cautiously: "So what do *you* think about this piece?"

I roll my eyes and counter abruptly, "Don't play Don Murray with me, asking me to talk about what I think before you do. I want to know what *you* think; I already know what I think." I am snappier than I expected to be. If he is going to trash my writing I'd rather get it over with already.

"I like the way you wrote it and I can find phrases in there to show you exactly where I liked it, but I guess," deep sigh, "I don't know enough about your new book. Why are you writing it? I don't understand the point of this piece. It feels like you took a small event and stretched it too far here, and I don't understand why you wrote it at all." He knows this is tough and he says it with tenderness, but I feel like the blasting caps were set and he just jumped on the trigger. I hear far more than he's said. The voice that always tells me I can't write begins the charge, *This is crap. Why would anyone write this? Forget revision—burn it.*

He dries his hands and comes to sit beside me on the couch in the kitchen nook. This man is my most gentle friend, but he is also an honest one; we both know my writing isn't going well. I feel a tear in my right eye trembling, ready to fall. Somehow I have mastered this technique of crying out of one eye only, the side away from my husband.

I manage to say, "This isn't helping," while I think, "I will never share another piece of my writing with you—EVER, and your hair is sticking up kind of funny this morning, too!" I reach for the Kleenex to honk loudly into a tissue. I've been ill for over a week now, a stuffy-head-fever misery that has gobbled up my entire winter break. My writing has been miserable in response. Perhaps it is the inability to think well when my head pounds and I empty one tissue box after the next. I am so tired, and writing takes energy and focus. I feel like I have nothing to say this week; I just want to curl up with a blanket and a good book. But I'm feeling the pressure of my August deadline as well. It's now December, true, but I have a lot of writing to do. It scares me.

Pat hasn't read my work for months. With my first book I brought draft upon draft to him, agonizing through the development of each essay, using his thoughtful reads to help me see what wasn't clear. It was *our* book most of the time. He was my first and most patient reader. And he played the role I needed: cheerleader. I was looking for that from him this morning, but I couldn't say it. I wanted him to focus on what was working in my piece and leave the problems for my own discovery because this was the first piece I'd written in a month that I felt had any promise at all. His response told me what I most feared: it was garbage. How could I go back to writing from there?

I knew, even as he was speaking, that this moment said something important about teaching writers to me. I could feel the frustration of my students when I talk to them about their work. I've seen the defiance; I've seen them crushed when I didn't mean to crush them. And I've listened for years to colleagues discussing how poorly kids write today. I've agreed with them. Clearly what we're doing in the teaching of writing is not working for too many kids. Too many leave high school unable to write clearly and confidently about anything—even the most important moments in their lives. I agree many aren't trying; they don't complete homework. They won't even step up to the plate. Since we're controlling the game, we have to ask ourselves, why not?

I think of our nights spent reading student papers and marking them, our days spent listening to experts and taking college courses, our hours of planning and calling parents, our willingness to work individually with students after school, and I wonder, why isn't it all working? Sitting on the couch in our kitchen looking at wintry grey skies out the windows on all sides, I got it.

Response is central to writing—we write to be heard and then wait eagerly to see if what was heard is what we intended. I brought my work to Pat and I needed encouragement, vision that I could get to the place I was looking for in my work. I knew there were problems in the piece, ones I'm sure Pat discovered. I should have explained what I was trying to do. Pat's instinct—Murray's teaching—was right. I needed to talk to Pat about the piece before he responded. He would have known how to speak about my writing in a way that would help me, if he'd listened first. But I responded to Pat just like my students do when I try this technique on them.

Tom, for instance, handed me his latest narrative draft last week and said, "Read this and tell me what you think."

I hesitated, then said, "Tell me about the piece, Tom. What do you feel is working? What isn't?"

He rolled his eyes, "I want *you* to tell *me* what you think! You're the teacher!" He doesn't say, but I can hear it clearly, *Do your job.*

I stood my ground and ignored his attitude. "I can help you better if you talk to me about the piece first. We only have a few more weeks together, Tom; you need to read your own work well and learn how to revise without me. It really is the most important thing I can teach you. Just tell me where you feel it needs work."

He reluctantly took the piece from me and started talking. Quickly I saw that he knew already what I was planning to tell him: where the structure fell apart. I needed to show him a way to flush out the focus because that would help him find a structure that was organized to make a point. If I hadn't listened first, our conference would have been a complete waste of time.

My response to my husband's reading told him I was in a precarious place as a writer and he stopped evaluating my work and just listened to me. But Pat and I have a relationship that is twenty years old and infinitely more complex than the ones I have with my students, so I was able to say, "This isn't helping," and he stopped talking. No student has ever stopped me to say this. Too often I trudge on correcting structure and incomplete arguments, and the student has stopped listening long ago. Writers put themselves on the page; we all do. When someone assaults that, it is personally painful. The wounded dog retreats to a cave, lesson over. You can keep talking, but no one is listening.

This scene in my kitchen really won't mark me as a writer. I'll get well and write with more energy; I'll be ready to hear Pat's honest read of my work. I have had enough success with my writing to believe somewhere inside that I really can do this, just not today. But how many of our students feel that way? For too many, the teacher is the sole authority on whether they write well or not. Not just for that piece, but for all time. They believe the teacher is evaluating their ability as a writer, not just evaluating that one piece of writing. And what they hear most of the time is that they don't write well. Teachers can be pretty severe readers: awk, frag, WW, ?, unclear! Too many teachers destroy any vision for the piece by evaluating the writing when it is still under development. It's a tiny chick pecking its way to the surface and we say, "That crack's all wrong."

I want excellence. I think every student should graduate from high school able to write clearly and confidently; I just disagree with how we're trying to get there. I know I can't write from a place of failure and frustration. I haven't gone back to the piece Pat read since that morning. I don't have the energy to fend off the voice hammering, *It's crap! Give it up!* Can you imagine the student who hears this about every piece they write? And don't fool yourself into thinking that a few hasty compliments before you start your evaluation make up for the hard punch to come. Pat tried that and I saw right through it. I knew what he really thought and our students do as well.

Confidence is everything. That tense, tight prose too many of my students write at the start of the year shouts of their insecurity with writing. Too many years with topics they couldn't care less about. They become first drafters, only drafters, weak writers, afraid to write.

Our students need readers who listen more than they talk. We need to listen, even when they resist this approach, because they have a lot of information about the development of the piece that helps us see what they need next as a writer. We waste our time when we only tell them what they already know about their writing. We need to show them what they don't see, and we'll never know what that is if we don't listen to them first.

Christine waved her paper in front of me two weeks ago, "This is draft *seven*, Mrs. Kittle," she said. Draft seven isn't there yet, but it is far from where she was on draft one. Had I tried to fix everything in that first draft, she probably wouldn't have bothered. Instead I chose one or two things at a time as I listened to her explain her goals for the piece. I kept encouraging her that this was an important piece. She did the rest.

It isn't easy to retrain ourselves—to read for what works and ignore the problems the first time we see a piece. If we try to remember that we are teaching a writer, not a piece of writing, it becomes easier. If we struggle to write ourselves, we begin to feel the importance of response. But what really matters—what's worth a few cartwheels on the front lawn—is that when we learn to respond well, our students will begin writing better.

confessions

Hope can be sold, it can be taught or at least spread,
it can survive in the strangest and most unlikely places.
It is a force that does not disappear.

—HERBERT KOHL

He's slight in build and pale, always. Nick's body type echoes his personality; he's a whisper in the halls. Onstage he is entirely different, brash and arrogant in one production, romantic and tender in the next, but always without concern for the impression he makes. He is simply a gifted, natural performer and he is truly at home onstage. I have always adored this kid because of his inner joy amid the cruelty and disdain of his peers. Nick has a small circle of friends who are loyal, but the greater population of the school snickers when he passes and scrawls his name on the bathroom walls. Nick is gay.

The day he tells me he says, "I think you probably already know this," and I nod, watching him watching me to see what I really think. Nick observes carefully, I've found; he sees between the lines. He tells me that he hasn't told his parents yet, but knows he has to.

I say, "Nick, I really believe your parents love you unconditionally, which means they'll love you just as much once they know."

God, I hope so. He flinches and I see the wave of emotion pass across his eyes, blurry and full and then clear again. He is fragile, sitting there framed against the darkened privacy glass of my office window. I continue, "Parents don't really have a choice about it, Nick; we love our children with a passion that frightens even us."

"Yeah," he agrees without conviction. "I know I have to tell them."

Last year Nick wrote an editorial for the school newspaper on the graffiti in the boys' bathroom in the A-wing. Written in black permanent marker, "Nick is gay" had shouted at all who entered. He had requested it be removed, but once painted over, it returned immediately. Bomb-threat graffiti was covered up within hours; to paint over gay slurs took a cycle of requests and scheduled maintenance time, although the implied threat, in my mind, was just as violent. One administrator kept a gallon of paint in his office so that he could paint over it himself as soon as it appeared. But we don't visit the bathrooms daily and Nick grew tired of reminding us.

The same students who tell me it is pretty cool that kids can come out at our high school will share the latest gay joke with their friends and howl with pleasure. Sure, you can come out, but we'll sneer at you for it and put your name into the jokes we tell. We won't tie you to the back of a pickup truck and drag you into a field, but we won't be seen with you, or partner up willingly with you in class, for fear this gay thing just might be contagious.

You're *out*, all right. Permanently.

O livia slumps on the couch in my study, her hands wringing in her lap and her eyes filling and spilling with tears. It is the same story, but in very different circumstances. Olivia is a first-year teacher struggling with the constant barrage of comments she overhears in the halls and in her room before the start of class. "You're gay; that's gay; don't be gay." She is.

She has come to my house on a Sunday night to tell me, and like Nick, watch how I might react to the news. She is frightened; I reassure her. But the issue is much bigger for her than this declaration to her supervisor. She wants my permission to come out to her students.

Just this week she had tried to discuss tolerance with her freshmen, responding to a student slur with her belief that being gay is not dirty or wrong or even all that important, but they had countered fiercely. When she said that according to statistics, one in ten students is likely a homosexual, Greg said, "Is anyone in this class gay? Put your hand up! Let's see." And it was all Olivia could do not to raise her own. She was unforgiving of her own hesitation and silence. What kind of role model was she?

There was the simple answer, of course: tell. I would stand beside her and field the parent concerns, defend her hiring with her teaching credentials and her passion for literature. But there was also the real possibility that the issue would consume her and the school, and she would be harassed, in our local paper, rejected loudly by the small-town community she had chosen as her home. Neither of us knew which way this might go.

Olivia took action. She proposed a support group for gay teens to our guidance director. The only word Olivia heard in their lengthy meeting was "discretion," a synonym for silence that Olivia knew well. Her mother had used it years ago, suggesting it would be better if Olivia moved out of state. The administrators suggested she have meetings at the fire station down the street so the group wouldn't appear to be "school sponsored."

Olivia resigned in the spring.

Thankfully, things have changed in the few years since that new teacher sat on my couch. Nick is a senior this year and he has gathered a support group, Common Ground, which is allowed to meet bimonthly right here in the building if they choose to. Students discuss gay and lesbian issues, form alliances with straight teenagers, and address issues of fairness and equity. It's a small step for our conservative, rural community, but a necessary beginning.

I met Nick in the main lobby as we waited for the final bell yesterday. We talked of graduation and his plan for college in the fall to study teaching. He told me he can't imagine having to hide who he is in order to teach music. He's afraid. He asks me, "Will things be different in four years?"

I can't say.

It's up to every one of us.

We say we want safe schools, but how badly, I ask you.

do the math

*Teachers are expected to reach unattainable goals
with inadequate tools. The miracle is that
at times they accomplish this impossible task.*

—HAIM GINOTT

My students file in from the hall as soon as home-room moves out, and the clock is on for me. In the passing time before class begins I put the agenda on the board, collect absence notes, and take attendance. Casual conversations help me gauge the day and check in with my kids, because the clock is ticking: ninety divided by twenty-four is under four minutes a kid per day; I've got to do a lot at once. I'm writing at the chalkboard and fielding questions when Krystal says behind me, "Mrs. Kittle, I found out last night that my dad has can-cer," her voice crumbling. She gathers her hair in both hands and looks away as I turn.

"Ah, Krystal," I stammer. "I'm so sorry."

"Thank you," she answers.

It is hard to be close to such grief; it is contagious.

"Can I turn my essay in on Monday?"

"Of course," I sigh.

The bell. The schedule's not up, but I have to begin. Teaching writing requires tremendous organization: models of great works, samples of my own process so they can find a path through a genre, and time with each student. I have to find a way to divide up my block-scheduled eighteen-week course into enough pieces to build trust with my students so they'll take risks and write well. I have to give them tools to improve their writing and enough encouragement so they'll believe they can. And I have to listen. I hand Krystal the tissue box. I know her family and had hoped so much for a different diagnosis. But the bell has rung; I'm already behind.

I realize I'm the envy of my colleagues in this country who teach English with classes of thirty, thirty-five, and more, but twenty-four is still too many. I can't get it all accomplished, not even close. Working with seniors, I focus on goals I believe are hugely important: preparing them for the rigor of college work; correcting errors in style, usage, structure, and support for an idea; providing vision for great writing through carefully chosen mentor authors such as Mitch Albom, Leonard Pitts, Jr., or Barbara Kingsolver. All this takes time. I have to help them find topics they can connect to, supportive organizers they need to break down the writing into parts, and the tools to analyze the craft of other writers so they can begin to build their own. The days disappear like parking spaces at the mall. I have fewer than nineteen minutes a week of class time per student, if there aren't any lost days from sickness, snow, suspension, family crisis, or family vacations.

In between teaching, department chair responsibilities, and my professional development work with new teachers in five schools, I glance at our local paper. A columnist is ranting about one of my new English teachers again; he calls him lazy. The paper chooses that sentence to bold and box to draw readers in, always anxious to start a fight. As I read I'm stunned at the outright lies, but the paper printed them and others will believe. As if teaching isn't hard enough already, I sigh. I know it is frustrating to be outside this big system we call school—judging its effectiveness by the few assignments brought home and the selected stories our children tell. But "lazy" keeps spinning in my mind long after I've put the paper aside. The columnist says teachers should be assigning and reading an essay a week from every student. Not a bad idea. I would like to, actually, but I don't know how it can happen.

I pull out my calculator; there's so much he doesn't understand. I assigned one essay every other week last semester and it just about crushed me. When the papers came in I read every one at least twice: once for content flow and an understanding of the writer's purpose, and then a second time to suggest, encourage, correct, and compare to the rubric we use for evaluation. When I was cooking—enough caffeine and quiet to be at maximum productivity—I could do all of that in ten minutes per essay, which times twenty-four students was four hours for one class. Most high school teachers carry four courses, so that is sixteen hours of reading and responding to just one essay per student per class. That isn't sixteen hours of misery by any means; student writing often delights and surprises me, but it is sixteen hours. There goes the weekend.

And the trouble is, that is on top of the fifty-hour work week already put in planning lessons and teaching them; staff, department, and committee meetings; parent phone calls (for discipline, attendance, or just concern, let alone to say how much I enjoy a child); parent meetings; professional development to retain my certification or address a district initiative; ordering supplies and books for my classroom; and then fitting in sporting events because I know how much they matter to my students. I add music performances and drama so that I can honor them all, but it adds up. If I'm really conservative here, I'd say that 7:00 A.M. to 4:00 P.M. barely covers all of that stuff. When you add another sixteen hours for reading those essays or other student work and my own professional reading (I subscribe to four journals), we easily have more than a sixty-hour work week. Thirty-eight weeks a year equals 2,280 hours total. Perhaps you know that a typical work year is 2,080 for fifty-two forty-hour weeks. Suddenly I know why I'm so tired all the time. This is why my husband complains that I fall asleep in my own drool when we rent a video to watch together. It's why we eat too many meals out, and I drink too much coffee. Add in the guilt I feel for Leaving a Child Behind—a truly haunting situation—and my cup just ran over.

There just isn't enough time to do all we believe is necessary in this work, not even close. I've done the math for twenty years now; I'd challenge that columnist to teach for even a week. We're in trouble in this profession and *we know it*. Needs are greater than ever, both emotionally and academically, so the kids seek more time than we have. But this is combined with a national teaching shortage. More than half of all new teachers leave education—for good—in the first three years of work. The talent I've seen pass through the doors of our school in the last five years is staggering. When we lose another teacher this spring, after hours of investment in helping him understand our curriculum and assessments and student population, will the rest of us have the stamina to keep going? Some years I wonder.

I wish I had more time in my day for students like Krystal. She's articulate and appreciative, one of those kids that keeps me going. Her dad was at graduation looking better than I expected, and I pray he will survive. But I also know this: if it were my daughter facing the loss of a parent, I'd want to believe that every adult in the school would take care of her, not just assign and grade her schoolwork. Teachers are called to do far more than deliver content to young minds; we need to shepherd kids to adulthood, sometimes because no one else can.

How do we find the time?

I'm honored to do this work, but I've done the math and it scares me.

It must be why I teach English.

a narrative in two voices

part I: the traffic cop

*If you watch closely enough, you can see the trajectory of
something dying long before the moment when we mourn its loss.
Like a football hurled deep downfield,
even in the process of its rising
we can sense the beginning of the fall.*

—MICHAEL JOHNSTON

"I am learning nothing in this class." Ken blurts this out loudly as I finish taking attendance. He has returned this morning from a five-day suspension for providing a junior high student with cigarettes. He passed them in an Altoids box as he cut through the cafeteria, but is furious he was caught. Even these five days later he is hostile, trying to convince me that if a kid wants to smoke, the adults really have no business getting in the middle of it. He glares at me from his desk nearest the door; his eyes are narrow and mean, his cheeks taut. He isn't fooling me, though; I know there's a kindness deep inside. The suspension cost him his quarter grades in several courses, and he can't make up the work. This has been the story of many of his failing grades since he began high school three years ago and he's grown tired of it. We all have. His dark hair falls in waves to his shoulders; his lips curl in a sneer as I ask him for his pass from the assistant principal. Ken, a student of remarkable brilliance, will not graduate from high school.

He's passing my class, but that doesn't earn me any points today. He missed my final test on *The Catcher in the Rye*. He had read the book and understood it at a deeper level than most of my other students, so I simply didn't figure the exam into his average. Perhaps that isn't fair to my other students, but the test would have been an exercise for him. I do not regret giving him a 73 for the quarter based on his complicated and rhythmic sonnets or his fluid, compelling essays, but after this angry pronouncement at the start of class, I want to plug in that test grade of zero and hope he fails. I glare at him sitting so smugly in his seat. I suddenly have a piercing pain in the center of my forehead, a product of little sleep, three mugs of coffee, and this.

Back off, Ken, if you know what's good for you, I glare silently back at him. My hostility surprises me. I like this kid. I truly do. But not today. Teachers have to teach, even when weak, ornery, and disillusioned.

Is it really me and my class that have produced this tirade from him? As my heart quickens I consider that he might be right. It is possible, I think, beginning to feel sick to my stomach. I could come up with a quick defense: he's lazy; he's a junior and repeating Freshman English for the third time; he's afraid to really make an effort. Excuses are such an easy and ready place to hide; I know teachers who make a career of it. I could send him back to the principal's office for his rudeness. At the intersection in my classroom this morning, with twenty cars approaching from all directions, Ken is weaving and swerving, lights flashing, horn blaring, determined to plow right through me.

He continues, "I learned much more from Mr. Fayle and Mr. Plese," spitting the words at me like miniature explosives. "You follow the curriculum too much. I am learning *nothing* in here." I smart at the mention of colleagues I believe know a tremendous amount about teaching writing. I'm not sure how to respond, embarrassed and unnerved at the eagerness of the other students to look at him, encouraging a fight, and my own growing fear that he's right.

As if to confirm it, I turn to the board and glance at my agenda, eager to start class. Literature analysis is first up on my list, a genre he'll likely never use in his real world of part-time jobs and a sketchy plan for college someday if he can pass the GED. What should I be teaching him instead? To love books, to write well, to read a text deeply for meanings that aren't seen at first glance. I know this, but I have a roomful of other students, most planning on going to college. The challenge is to direct them all smoothly onward, even though Ken is determined to crash.

Near the end of the semester Ken volunteers to read his book review. I cringe. I value his facility with language but I haven't forgotten his reckless assault on my teaching and have no wish to repeat it. I trust in something I've seen in him before, though; he understands literature well.

"I have read *Of Mice and Men* three years in a row now," he begins with a smirk. My students snicker and sit up a little straighter. "It gets better every time and is, perhaps, the best book I've ever read in my life." The stillness in the room is the only appropriate response. He continues reading, his words succinct and poignant, comparing the affection of George for his surrogate brother Lenny, in the novel, to his own mother's care and protection of him throughout his war with school. Ken thinks deeply about all things, I know, but I'm surprised that he is sharing this with a room of students two years younger than he is, none of them his friends.

But then I get it. Ken knows this moment matters. He has few credits and the rest of the cars are shifting into higher gears. He won't find a ready audience for his articulate and sensitive views on life. Or his tirades. He completes his review by saying that every student should read Steinbeck's novel—that teachers should *make* them, even if they don't want to—his eyes glancing at mine and a smile spreading across his face. I grin back.

"I will, Ken," I say, but we both know it isn't that simple. The first two times he read the novel begrudgingly, and he didn't learn much. It is the student who makes learning happen. We can try to force them through school, but their resistance is stronger.

I'm leaping to the curb after my sprint through light traffic in front of our school when I next see Ken, several months later. He beams at me and shouts, "Hey, Mrs. Kittle!" It's clear he is happier, the tension gone from his forehead and his shoulders. His eyes sparkle a deep blue in the midday light.

I pause and say warmly, "I haven't seen you in so long. Where have you been?"

"I dropped out," he says, still smiling, "but I'm working on my GED. and then I'm going to college! I knew you'd like that."

"You're right," I reply with a smile, "I'd love to see you go to college." He continues walking down the street and I return to my pursuit of a sub sandwich.

"Take care, Ken."

"See ya, Mrs. Kittle."

a narrative in two voices

part II: Ken's story
by Ken Fowler

*R*eturning from a week's long suspension, I remember the feeling of despair as I shuffled into first period. Mrs. Kittle's Freshman English could have been my favorite class, if not for the fact I was a junior. It was my third time through the program. Like the immature punk I was, I had not learned from previous mistakes. Not only academically, but also socially, I continued down a misguided road. I had given an underclassman cigarettes, which is not only against school policy, but illegal as well.

Feeling the punishment undeserved I came back from serving my "sentence" ready to lash out at the "establishment." I was looking for a fight that morning. When Mrs. Kittle obliged me, I jumped at the chance. I lit into her like a shot from a gun: first casting her teaching style in doubt among my fellow students, then comparing her unfavorably to former teachers. Seeing her reaction of surprise and anger I knew I had won this round against the powers that be. Almost immediately I regretted my attack, knowing that her job would be that much harder with the rest of the class. Not until much later would I realize how dumb my actions were. Upperclassmen should be an example to the younger students. They should not take away from them.

High school was a never-ending misery. It was a constant struggle just to make it through the day. I dreaded waking up in the morning. If there wasn't a conflict with the administration, there was a fight with one of my fellow students. Trying to find my identity during this time was harder than pulling teeth. The quiet studious type was never my bag. So I tried the troubled intellectual. That however never worked either. I wanted to fit in too much to follow that path far. Finally I fell into the stereotype of last resort, which by my third go at Freshman English I had down pat. I was the class clown and troublemaker. My conflict with teachers was legendary. My profane vocabulary was the widest around. Foolishly, I was proud of these things. I was proud to call the vice principal's office and Social Restriction a second home. I was prouder still of the ability to avoid education at any cost.

In trying to gain social acceptance I became a self-imposed exile. I was trying to be the original bad boy. I succeeded in becoming a generic punk. As the class clown I failed to realize that my peers weren't laughing with me but laughing at me.

I've since talked to many teachers I came in conflict with during my school days. Then I thought them arrogant tyrants, now I find them unique individuals who must deal with a few bad apples to give the rest of today's youth a chance. Who would have thought?

You know I never thought English class would ever affect my life after high school. In a weird twist of fate I spend almost every day with books. Now I must say Mrs. Kittle and those teachers that came before her taught me invaluable lessons about literature that I couldn't live without. High school just wasn't for me. I could give you any number of reasons. But in the end it's intangible why so many succeed where I failed. But I live my life with no regrets. Always trying to get ahead and I often do. Then Murphy's Law will take effect and I will be right back where I started. But I am happy with my chosen profession and my life as a whole, something I never thought would happen.

In retrospect I owe high school and those teachers who helped shape my perceptions a thank-you. Who knows, I might even go to college, get my teaching degree, and let ironic fate take its course.

one large to go, extra cheese

Human existence is more stubborn and resilient than we know. There is a toughness in our kind, an adaptability and tenaciousness that keeps us scrabbling up toward sunshine against all odds.

—LEONARD PITTS, JR.

I saw her at the pizza place on the highway last summer. I knew her immediately: same pretty face and short, light-brown hair. She was in charge, shuffling orders and holding the phone against one ear while she slid a large pizza into the cardboard box. "Grab dinner and get home" was all I was thinking before I saw her. Would she remember me? I smiled when she turned her attention my way. "Hey, Brandi," I said.

"Hey, Ms. Kittle." She paused in her hustle and said nothing for a moment while the door opened behind me and two more pizzas came out of the oven to drop right in front of her. "How you doing?"

"How are *you* doing, Brandi, I haven't seen you in forever." I was really asking about *her*, but I guess I knew my question implied her absence from school, how she'd dropped out years before. I don't measure the worth of kids by whether they stay in high school, but as an agent of the system I'm sure most believe I do. She looked at me carefully.

"I got my GED," she said with just a touch of self-assurance and spunk, cutting slices with the pizza wheel spinning beneath her hands.

"Good for you; I bet you did." I smiled. This girl was going to make it—of course she was.

"Yeah, and I'm doing good. I have a daughter."

I smiled. "I bet she's adorable. What's her name?"

That's one area I knew she was well prepared for. When she was in my language arts class she was already mothering two younger brothers with a confidence I couldn't understand. I only found out about her home life because she was late to school so many times that I finally said, "Why can't you get here by 7:25?", my exasperation evident.

She returned fire. "Because I have to get my brothers breakfast and dressed and ready for school!" Her eyes were defiant, her jaw set.

"Where's your mom?"

"She's working. She works nights. She doesn't get home until *after* 7:30."

So she came in late and I quit marking her tardy. She was in school almost every day. She couldn't do homework because Mom was sleeping once she got home from school and little boys were a lot of work; did I know that? I did.

I helped her finish eighth grade, but in the end Brandi didn't finish high school. We have this romance with homework in America. And Brandi had attitude, spunk, a need to survive. She didn't suffer fools or listen to lectures; she'd tell a teacher off before she'd explain what was going on. And before you judge this girl too harshly, go and try it for a few weeks: raise yourself and two siblings, and manage six teachers and study guide questions on a dead president, for Pete's sakes, and then sit in another detention because you were late to school—when wouldn't it have been worse to leave those two boys home alone? And no, there wasn't anyone else who could help with child care and few people who really understood. Brandi has a good heart. She was bright and lively at fourteen. We dropped her into that hole of disobedience: tardy, confrontational, suspended.

She was determined and she crawled out—by her own force of will. I admire that.

I cradled my pizza and passed the twenty across the counter. "It was so good to see you," I said. I wish I'd said a lot more.

She answered, "You, too. Take care, Ms. Kittle."

Then Matt appeared at my office door on Friday. He said he just wanted to say good-bye, since it was his last day of school.

"You did it," I grinned, offering my open hand for a high five.

"Yeah, it's kind of embarrassing when you think about it. I'm twenty years old and still in high school. But I finished," he snickered.

"You came back, Matt. That's fabulous. Most kids don't. You have to be proud of that."

"I know. Most of my friends just didn't bother. I figured it was only one math class; I might as well." He gave me a shy grin, blue eyes peeking out from under his baseball hat, hands in his pockets. I smiled, remembering how many times I badgered him to return to school as he sent my groceries across the scanner the summer before. "Come on, Matt, one class. You have to finish," I'd say.

Always polite, he'd smile and say, "Maybe," but I didn't think he would. Once kids start working it is hard to snatch them back from steady paychecks. I promised to help if he'd give it a try. We'd gotten to know each other the fall before when I had him in an American Literature course for juniors and seniors. I kept him near the front of the class to help with his hearing problem, which meant we had a lot of conversations at the start of class. Matt wrote once that he hadn't had his hearing aid in several months. His dog had chewed it up and a new one cost $850. Since he let the dog get at it, his parents said he had to replace it. Matt said he missed hearing birds; when he first had his hearing corrected he just couldn't believe the sound of them. There wasn't a trace of whining in his writing, just an explanation for why he didn't always follow what I was doing in class.

This is when I love this work; here was something I could fix.

Armed with his journal I went to see his guidance counselor. I asked him to set up a meeting with Matt's mother. I figured Matt hadn't explained how much he needed the hearing aid to learn. If his parents knew, I figured they'd replace it.

The following week his mother was seated in one of those stiff plastic chairs with her back to the wall when I came in; Matt sat across from her. I shook her hand and thanked her for coming in. She smiled thinly. I explained that Matt's struggle in my class was at least partially due to his missing hearing aid. She said, "I don't know if he told you, but he let the dog chew that up."

"Yes," I answered, "he told me. How frustrating."

"It's eight hundred and fifty dollars to replace it and that's his responsibility; I told him that. I don't have eight hundred and fifty dollars." She was matter-of-fact, serious, but resigned. She stayed stiffly against that chair, clearly uncomfortable. This wasn't open for discussion. There are many families that just can't handle a loss of that much cash. I came from one; I remember.

Matt said, "You're right, Mom." I watched him smile at her.

"And he's working, but he spends his money on his truck instead," she nodded at him.

"You're right, Mom, I do." Matt grinned at all of us and ducked his head beneath his hat. I wanted to beat my head against my desk in frustration. No wonder he was failing math, and I was out of ideas.

Joe, the counselor, had been in guidance for years. He jumped in. "You know, Social Security might cover it. I have the forms; we could apply. It's worth a try."

Yes! I would never have thought of this. I often need my colleagues to help me figure out a problem, but I forget to ask them. I don't know why I try to be the Lone Ranger, but it is a definite weakness of mine. Within weeks Matt's hearing aid was in his ear. Problem was, it was late spring and he still failed math. It was too late. When the rest of the class graduated, he stayed home.

That summer, I worked on him every week when I shopped for groceries. He was taking algebra as a correspondence course, but he couldn't learn it on his own. I offered to help. (Actually, I volunteered my math-wizard husband to help, but don't tell him.) But Matt didn't call. He failed the course and fumed at the waste of money.

I kept at him: "School is free; come back."

And then one morning that fall, there he was. I stopped in my tracks as I came through our main lobby. It was 7:15 and he was back in school, waiting for class. I shook his hand. What a kid. He came faithfully to his math class all semester and marched with the others on Saturday. My heart soared when he came toward the stage, wearing the same shy smile, but this time it was dipped beneath a stiff black hat and a tassel was brushing his cheek. I gave him a thumbs-up when he passed my seat. It was his quiet journey; none of his friends were there. They forgot his name in the program even, which made me crazy, but Matt probably didn't care. He finished; that's what mattered.

When I'm feeling low, wondering why so many kids can't complete high school, I remember Brandi and Matt. They found their own way.

multigenre marriage

It is with true love as it is with ghosts;
everyone talks about it, but few have seen it.

—FRANÇOIS DE LA ROUCHEFOUCAULD

*M*y teaching life has always spilled into my personal life. This year love became curriculum, an odd but appropriate match, when the last day before holiday break fell on our twentieth wedding anniversary. It was the romance of a few snowflakes falling on my way to class, reminding me of the night we were married; it was students slurping on candy canes, sitting on top of the desks and not there to learn, obviously. It was me, holding on, counting the minutes until class would be over, and my husband Pat slipping in through the door while I was talking. He stood quietly watching for a bit and then asked if he could have a few minutes with my students. I noticed his leather portfolio in one hand.

"Oh no," I said. "You're not going to embarrass me again."

Emma brightened up, asking, "Are you going to sing?"

He walked to the front as he smiled at her and said, "No, no singing," but he was taking off his coat. The kids buzzed with possibility; Pat's serenade on a previous anniversary was well known. He looked at me. "I just need an overhead projector."

"Sorry, this room doesn't have one," I said. I felt a little sorry and a little relieved.

"Well," and he turned to face the front of the room, where the one I hadn't noticed sat on the floor, "I called ahead and ordered one. I've prepared a multigenre project that I want to share with your students, if that's okay." He had to be joking. My husband's a chemical engineer, a small-business owner, and my best friend in the world, but a multigenre writer? He continued, "See, Penny talks about you guys all of the time. And she's been talking about these multigenre projects you're doing, like how Tim was doing his on poop, but he changed his mind."

Tim laughed.

"So I decided to try to write one for our anniversary."

I leaned forward, flashing a warning look at him. "On what?" I finally managed.

"You," and he smiled that mischievous grin that made my heart thunder when we were both seniors at Oregon State University. My students all turned my way. I heard Jon say, "Oh, YES!"

"Oh no," I sighed, "this is going to be way too much information for this class." But no one was listening; all eyes were on him. I found a seat at the back of the room on a student desk.

"Mrs. Kittle, did you know he was coming?" Liz whispered down the row of desks.

"No—I figured he was here to pick me up for our trip, that's all."

"Look how red she is," Sabrina called from across the room.

Pat had papers and color overheads in his portfolio and he was arranging them on a desk. "Do you guys mind if I share this with you?"

Well, you can imagine what they said.

And so it began. First a memoir: our first date. It's funny how writing reveals all kinds of things that haven't been said. Pat wrote about feeling shy and thinking I was distracted, looking for someone better. *It wasn't like that at all*, I wanted to interrupt, *I was just nervous*, but for once I just listened. And remembered.

Next was research. He said he knew it was a requirement of our projects and that he had tried to research marriage but it was just so boring, all of those facts and figures. So instead he decided to research Penny Ostrem, the girl I was before we were married. "Then it was easy," he said to my students. "It was fun." I was grateful for this model of a writer's process shared so naturally with my students.

Pat began with an overhead of me at five years old, standing next to a giant Pooh bear I still have somewhere in the basement. He chronicled my early interests and then switched photos. Blown up on the overhead projector, my wire-framed-stop-sign-shaped-dork-of-the-year-junior-high-school picture spanned half of the wall. Pat filled them in on my hippie attempts of 1974, complete with embroidered shirt, full set of braces, and long, blonde hair. After the laughter dulled a bit, several called out at once, "Are those the glasses?"

"Yes, those are them," I admitted. I had been working on my own multigenre project for the last few weeks with this class: a project on 1974, the year I turned thirteen. I had told my class about my desperate attempts to be cool: my crush on Elton John; my best friends; the stolen cigarettes we sneaked behind the pine trees that lined the playground at our K–8 school. And yes, how I'd faked poor vision at an eye exam in order to get those glasses because I needed them for the whole "look."

The next photos were from high school cheerleading and varsity tennis. "Nice shorts," Krista remarked, grinning into her collar, setting off a chorus of laughs.

"I know," I said and rolled my eyes. "It was a long time ago."

"No kidding," she smirked.

Pat previewed the next slide with a few comments about my undesirable friends I found in college. *No party pictures*, I prayed. Teachers walk that careful line between honesty and being a role model when teaching high school: there is much I don't tell. But the photo was of me and Captain Hook at Disneyland on April break. Phew. He followed it with our wedding photo and said, "I was so lucky that she said yes," causing a little sweep of *aaaaahh*s to pass down the line of girls at the back.

There was a history of my teaching career told in captions, and then a poem about our nightly walks in our neighborhood, which he introduced by saying it was the first poem he'd ever written in his life, but that his writing coach, Don Graves, had insisted he give it a try.

"Don helped you?" I yelped.

"Yes, I called him up and told him I needed a writing conference and he let me come up to his house. I had no idea what multigenre was and I certainly couldn't ask you!" And again—there it was. What do writers do in the process of creating a piece that matters to them? They find other writers to confer with. I couldn't have scripted this. One teacher's voice day after day grows tiresome to kids. I love it when they hear my lessons from another teacher, another voice, another writer. And all were listening even as the clock ticked toward the last few moments of class.

Pat saw me glance at my watch and said, "How much time do we have?"

Matt, the one most ready to leave each day, said quickly, "Take *all* the time you need." I couldn't help but grin.

Pat's next piece was a recipe for marriage. He said he'd heard me talking one night about the recipes my students had played with one day: a recipe for an anorexic; a recipe for an adolescent boy; a recipe for fighting cancer. He started reading.

Recipe for a Marriage

Ingredients vary, but according to the Bush administration must include one man and one woman. Some ingredients gel instantly upon contact, while others require significant mixing to achieve the right conditions for marriage.

Place one man and one woman in close proximity to one another, but take pains to keep them separated. Add a dash of flirtation to the woman, and a pinch of shyness to the man, and allow the two to set for a period of time, exchanging furtive glances. Mix the two together in a social situation and observe the reaction. If needed, mix repeatedly in a variety of social situations until the ingredients begin to blend together.

Beating of the ingredients is counterproductive, and always results in a bad marriage.

Once the ingredients have blended sufficiently together, add a large helping of love. They are now ready for marriage.

Preheat oven to hot, add a layer of physical intimacy to the ingredients, and bake at high temperatures. Repeat baking process frequently during early years of marriage.

"Stop!" I called. "No more baking!" The kids were howling.

"Mrs. Kittle," John said, "you are going to be hearing about this for a VERY long time." And several others added, "Oh, yeah." And I deserved it. I had needled John for days after I walked by him and his girlfriend lip-locked in the cab of his pickup truck during the homecoming bonfire in September.

"Let him finish," someone said. Pat grinned and continued.

After baking, allow to cool, then remove from container and immediately apply support to the mixture or it will fall. Some typical examples of support are sharing of household chores, allowing your partner to pursue their career or schooling, and sharing child-rearing duties.

Frost entire marriage with joy and mutual respect for each other.

The worst part about this recipe is, despite how good the marriage looks, it is never quite finished. Every marriage is a work in progress.

The best part of this recipe is that there is lots of baking involved.

After the snickers and cheers died out, Pat shared his final piece, a letter. I could feel the tears starting as he stood there before my students and said, "You are the complete package, the whole enchilada, the real deal. You are my best friend and the only woman I want to share my life with. Happy twentieth anniversary. Love, Pat." I managed to join the collective sigh of appreciation from my class and clapped loud and long.

Pat nailed it: the whole multigenre thing. How one subject written about in one form is limited, but when you open up your thinking to write in many different genres, you open up the subject in ways even you, the writer, hadn't imagined. Your readers experience your subject from many angles and walk away with an understanding, not just a reading. If Pat had done only the research piece, even with entertaining photos, my students would know a little more about *me*, but little about *Pat and me*, which was his inspiration for writing. If they had heard only the poem, they'd have missed the playfulness that I adore in his recipe. Multigenre allows for complex thinking about our complex lives.

Of course, there's plenty I wish he hadn't left my students thinking about. Two girls came out the door behind us as we left class that day, and Liz said, "Have a nice trip, Mrs. Kittle, and don't do too much baking over the holidays!" which left them giggling while a furious color returned to my cheeks. You can bet that blush won't be the last one.

Our multigenre projects have been a burst of energy during a distracted time of year. It's all about the investment of self in writing: when my students choose topics they care about, they bring excitement and interest to class, even in December. Writing assignments that travel from one frozen style to another handcuff writers. We dictate form and narrow the subject matter for them. We copy templates and determine the font size. Then their stiff prose leaves us yawning and procrastinating about reading their work, and it is rarely their best. Over the last few weeks twenty-six different multigenre projects have emerged in my room: Nicole has chronicled her battle with anorexia; Taylor has pulled together hours of research on LSD; Christina has illuminated her obsession with the UNH men's hockey team; Heidi has mesmerized us with the history of the tango. She promises to teach it to the class during her presentation. I've been waiting to see these final products come together, excited to have them in my hands. I need that kind of energy in my classroom.

When I came down the aisle in white to Pachelbel's Canon in D Major, I couldn't see how multifaceted the years ahead would be— wondrous, rich, and at times, heartbreaking. It was looking into the blue eyes of our son Cam after a long and frightening night of labor; it was trying to call Pat's mom back from a coma. It was Hannah's triumphant first ride on her bike; it was Pat in a tuxedo promising to love me always. Multigenre writing helps me and my students find a way to hold it all. And share.

score

Winning is almost everything.

—JIM LOY

I checked the sign-up list in the main office after class. I was looking for an excuse to erase my name from the faculty Powder Puff football team. See, I'd kind of gotten myself into a hole with a couple of students in class, boasting that the faculty team was going to wipe the floor with the seniors. Now I regretted it. I wanted out.

My perky signature stood alone, just one name on a long, empty page. Sixty-three staff members, more than half women, and no one was playing; I couldn't believe it. Powder Puff football is a main event at Kennett High School in the fall. It is part of our Homecoming Week celebration that includes a parade on Main Street with folks lined up for blocks to watch the kids come by. Generations have grown up in the halls of our school, and it's worth celebrating. We have a final assembly on Friday, and the girls from each class compete in front of the student body to be Powder Puff champions. These chicks are serious. For weeks they practice with guys they pick as coaches. They are on the field after school running plays, learning positions, practicing strategy. The girls train with passion and grit, sweat darkening their terry cloth headbands. And then in the final few minutes of the assembly, the winners take on a ragtag faculty team just to show how much better they are than their tired old teachers. Every year I agree to quarterback; every year we lose. Badly.

Oh, I get it, *that's* why no one signs up.

But this year I had made it worse than the others. I had Carrie and Katelyn in first block, two of the strongest athletes in the senior class. They knew I'd be playing, so every morning they taunted me, "Mrs. Kittle, we're going to annihilate you."

And I'd come back with "You two are going down! I'll see to it myself." Now these girls are beautiful and smart, and you can't help but love them, but they are also fierce competitors. Blonde hair swinging, lips curled back in a sneer, I could imagine them crouched before me waiting for the rush; I started to get nervous. They would knock me over and laugh as they helped me up. Yes, they would.

I tried recruiting staff in the halls between classes, in the bathroom, in the lunch line, on my way out to the parking lot. Hmmmm, she looks like a linebacker. "Wanna play Powder Puff?" I'd say. I got that snorting kind of laugh from most, then fielded a few grumbles about wasting our time on this Spirit Week stuff; Mrs. Bates said the assembly was cutting into her lesson plans. I looked away so she wouldn't see me roll my eyes. Friday arrived and I had no one. The gym began to fill, the band blasted our fight song, and I ran from bleacher to bleacher begging colleagues to help me out.

"Come on, Kara, I know you're a runner."

"I don't play football," she said, but she seemed a little sorry.

I smiled at her, but my eyes growled. "No one expects us to *play*," I said as I glanced to others nearby. "Catie? Becky? You two can pretend, right?" They hesitated—ha! I moved in closer to take advantage of my first-year teachers. "Please?" I used my sweetest, most desperate voice.

"I really can't do this," Catie said, but she moved out onto the floor, Becky close behind. Yes. We convinced Kara and rounded up three others as the stands pulsed with the noise of nine hundred teenagers. The boys in football shirts lined the gym, arms crossed, sizing up the girls in shorts and personalized team jerseys practicing out on the floor. I looked at my small band of comrades and we were a sorry-looking excuse for a team. We had borrowed tennis shoes, no confidence or matching T-shirts. We didn't even have a coach.

I grabbed my writing buddy Ryan Mahan, hoping he might help us organize, and it was a smart choice; he knew plays. Ryan is a bundle of frantic, new-teacher energy, never afraid to make a fool of himself—or others, I imagined, listening to his plans with trepidation, I must admit. He started gesturing about offense and man-to-man coverage and I watched my young recruits' eyes lose focus. This was an entirely different language; we were definitely in trouble.

Theresa offered, "How about a long bomb?"

"Yeah," I said, "we can pull that off," glancing at our adversaries lined up just outside our huddle, one long line of bobbing ponytails. Black greasepaint decorated their pale cheeks. The coaches called them by line and position and they sprang to the floor. But it was more than readiness, they had jump. I felt all of my forty-two years just watching them.

"What's a long bomb?" Catie leaned over to ask me, a perplexed look in her eyes.

Excellent. *We are toast*, I sighed.

The screeches of bare skin against a polished floor and the rumbling shouts from the stands forced our attention to that first game: the freshmen and juniors in a lively battle. On the next play there was a tangle of bodies on the floor, and I watched both Catie and Becky take a step backward. Meanwhile I scanned the stands for my son. He's a sophomore. I spotted him sitting with his friends, who are all sports fanatics. I groaned. It won't be pretty; sorry, Cam.

The juniors scored and then let the clock run out. Leaping into the arms of their coach, they headed to the sidelines to await the outcome of the next game. The freshmen bowed their heads and found their seats in the stands.

Halftime. Ed Fayle organized his Blues Brothers cheerleaders for their annual performance. Eight male teachers in black pants, white shirts, thin black ties, dark shades, and Ed with a whistle. They marched to the center of the gym and began a wacky cheer. It included stork poses, booty shakes, and pointing at the crowd. The students giggled and hooted at our sixty-eight-year-old substitute coordinator, his pants held at the waist by wide swaths of silver duct tape. Next minute he was on his back like a turtle and he needed help getting up. Laughter rocked the bleachers.

The sophomores and seniors began round two. Katelyn and Carrie were dominant. Becky turned to me, saying, "I don't want to play the seniors; those girls are scary." No kidding.

The seniors won easily, but the juniors came out on fire for the final game. They were well-organized and fearless. Two quick touchdowns and the seniors went down, surprisingly crushed by the smaller, faster juniors. I had no time to feel sorry for Katelyn and Carrie, though; we were on. Three minutes of playing time. *How bad can it be?* I jogged out to the center of the floor, my team following. The jeers from the crowd began immediately.

"Long bomb," I said to Theresa as we huddled just beyond the scrimmage line. I eyed the juniors as they motioned for position, snickering as they looked us up and down. Suddenly I wanted to crush them. I'm afraid I might've even snarled in their direction.

We broke at the whistle and lined up for the hike. Lindsay crouched low with the ball, Catie and Becky stood at my side. A line of juniors, just a few feet before me, were poised for the charge. They looked surly.

"You guys, block the rush," I said quickly to my rookies.

"What's a rush?"

"How?"

I couldn't explain; Gary, our head football coach, was about to blow the whistle for the play.

In the stands my son's friend Jamie said to him, "Oh look, Cam, it's your mom as quarterback. Can she even throw?"

"I don't think so," said Cam, and shook his head. Jamie offered him a grin.

At the whistle Lindsay put the ball in my hands and the juniors lunged forward. I darted to the left (evading the blockers, my son told me later) as I looked for Theresa, off in a sprint toward the end of the gym. She was moving. I pulled back and felt all the throws of my childhood as my arm released the ball. I was always the tomboy, playing football and basketball with neighbor kids until dark. I learned how to wrap my fingers around the laces and spin a spiral farther and farther across the field; I begged to be picked as quarterback. And today this throw was flying! It felt like I'd sent it too far, but it was beautiful as its arc spanned the length of the gym, drawing the eyes of most spectators in imitation of its path. We all watched its perfect flight. Theresa reached out in front of her, small arms ready for the catch. Somehow it was there, and she snatched it close, making a final leap into the end zone, flags waving from her waist, just out of reach of those pesky teenagers.

Score!

The crowd went wild. Well, okay, only the teachers really, but they were on their feet with their arms in the air, celebrating. My student Tanner had the microphone, taping commentary for our local TV station. He said, "Mrs. Kittle, *oh my God*. That was like a sixty-yard pass!" Oh yes, sweet, sweet victory. Carrie and Katelyn rushed out on the floor to give me high fives and the rest of my students joined in, a line of smiling faces and looks of disbelief as I twirled and danced and jumped across the floor. Gary blew his whistle in celebration; our principal pumped his fist in the end zone; Ryan was doing a boogie dance on the sidelines and shaking his head.

Final score 7-nothing.

We were the champions.

I passed through crowds of kids that afternoon high-fiving students from years past and laughing with colleagues who shook their heads in disbelief. It was exhilarating to come out on top after all those years.

But you've probably figured out this story is about more than winning.

I once noticed that the crowd of students in the halls of our school can feel much like the anonymity of a busy city street. We're all in a hurry; there's never enough time. Heads bob along as a crush of bodies and motion forces us all to focus on negotiating our way through instead of noticing each face in front of us. In our hallways and on the stairs and across the main lobby to the crush in the cafeteria I regret not knowing all these kids that pass by me silently, heads down, eyes watching the feet before them.

But it changed when I threw that pass. There were moments of recognition, connections, like a few days later when I was off to pick up mail in the office. Classes were buzzing behind each door as I moved through the wide corridor, empty and shining in the morning light. From around the corner came a kid, a backpack dragging him lopsided as he found his way to class or the nurse's office or (I can always hope!) the library. Our eyes met. I could feel the start of the polite, half-smile of a stranger, but he didn't just glance away, he said, "Hey, Brett Favre, nice pass," and playfully raised his eyebrows my way.

"Oh," I replied with a grin as we stopped a few feet apart. "You were there?"

He nodded.

"I couldn't believe it; could you?" I asked.

"Uh, no, not really." I love that honesty in adolescents. He broke into a grin that filled his face; I almost saw teeth. Our laughter bounced across the empty hall and dribbled down the stairs to run up against those closed classroom doors and pass like fog might under the door frame and through the space at each hinge. He left me smiling. I don't even know his name, but we shared something.

Suddenly this city doesn't feel quite so lonely anymore.

ending

*For every gardener knows that
after the digging, after the planting,
after the long season of tending and growth,
the harvest comes.*

—MARGE PIERCY

"What? Are you crying?" My principal turns to notice my red face as the fading notes of the senior video resound in the auditorium around us. I shake my head, but I can't hide it. It's early Sunday morning as Project Graduation comes to an end, and I'm a mess. I wish I could stop myself, I'm feeling more joy and pride than sadness, but I've figured out it is just part of who I am: when it comes to good-byes, I'm liquid. The seniors begin to file out and each one stops to shake Jack's hand. They say, "Good-bye, Mr. Loynd, thank you." I'm glad they recognize his dedication; he's an inspiring leader. I cower behind him, though, trying to avoid this ending with these kids.

It doesn't last for long.

"Mrs. Kittle?" I turn and it's Timmy White, bleach-blond hair and that shy smile with his hand out, saying "Thank you for everything." Yeah, you'd be crying too. Little Timmy, who was so silent in my eighth grade that I wondered if he'd ever break out, became the king of mountain biking and confidence. I loved it when he dyed his hair and became a defining captain of our hockey team. Tim is taller than I am now and off to college, and I got to watch it happen. He came back through the line just to say thanks. Boy, I'll miss him.

Tanner is careful to shake all of our hands and offer thanks. He's been a joy to coach in writing. I love this kid: his sense of humor, his perseverance, and his kindness. The video we watched was produced by his mother, Theresa, and it was filled with footage from preschool parades, elementary school, family photos and then homecoming, senior prom, and even graduation, but when it was spliced together you could see how fast it goes, from the first bus ride to kindergarten to the tossing of black caps into a blue sky. We only have them for a few moments and then they are gone. This is the hardest part about being a teacher: at some point you just have to let them go.

Close on Tanner's heels is Torin. I'm sniffling again even before he reaches out to give me a tight hug. He says, "You know we'll still see each other." I do know, but it won't ever be like this. Torin was always bouncing in his seat in my language arts class at age twelve. He even bounced as he wrote, so full of joyful energy he couldn't contain himself. Lanky and tall, I knew he'd command the baseball field by senior year. None of us expected leukemia, chemotherapy, and a frail frame pausing before a set of two stairs to collect his strength on his way to class. This was a long year, but Torin has made a slow recovery. He's off to study journalism and I'll miss watching him from afar, willing him to be well. I'll miss reading his stories, correcting his punctuation, and telling him to quit talking. I'll just miss him.

I didn't see several others. On purpose. I would have hugged them and leaked my blubbery nose all over their shoulders. I know that Adam and Kyle are off to the air force and we are a country at war; I can't say good-bye. I know Carrie, Katelyn, and Krystal helped me believe in myself as a teacher when I was filled with doubt, and I don't know exactly how to thank them. I know that Cathleen's graduation was a gargantuan force of will, more than most adults I know would be capable of, considering all she had to overcome. I know too many kids who have desperately ill parents who may not be here to guide them much longer. Teaching has allowed me to counsel and encourage kids, but mostly just to listen to them, laugh with them, and enjoy them.

I watched the students sprint to their cars in the early morning light and then listened to peeling tires on Main Street. "See ya, Mrs. Kittle!" Matt yelled out his window with a wave, roaring the engine of his battered pickup truck. I smiled and called one last "Be careful," which I'm sure he ignored.

I carried half-empty cups of coffee to the trash. I slapped each theatre seat upright and discovered donut remains on paper plates, a few napkins, and one gym bag full of clothes. When I made it all the way to the front near the stage I turned back and looked at the seats, dark and silent, row upon row. They seemed so empty. Waiting. They need that next bunch of loud teenagers to fill them up.

I'm waiting, too.

I'm already looking over my class list for the fall and imagining beginning again. I can't predict that experience: which essays will inspire me, which stories my students will bravely tell, which experiences will leave us howling with laughter. My classroom will be filled with wonder, frustration, and joy; I'm sure of it. I know I will love my new students fiercely, more than most folks would say I should. I will cry when they leave. Every year. How could I do it any differently?

Teaching pulses with rhythm. Each summer an ending with kids I've grown to love. Each fall a beginning when anything is possible. Twenty years ago when I stood before my first class of students I didn't know if I'd make it to the end of the day. I still feel that way sometimes. But I also love the discovery, the challenges, and the kids. Especially the kids.

I am a teacher.

This water is magical, dimpled with light.

In the midst of darkness there will always be a dawn, and a reason to keep trying.

I don't catch them all, but I try to give each one something to take downstream: a few stories they'll remember with a smile, the tools and habits of a writer, and the steady, sure belief in who they are and who they can become.

afterword

*W*hen a teacher gazes at a junior high or high school classroom of twenty-five to thirty students, she or he is looking out over kids with a range of experiences. There are students who have been sexually mistreated: one in three girls, one in five—or seven, depending on which numbers you accept—boys. One in ten of the students is homosexual, and therefore prone to secrecy for the sake of survival. Who knows how many others have been diminished by power struggles until their self-esteem has been elbowed aside by temper or, worse, depression? And how many have simply never been allowed to be good enough by parents who believe debasement is the best way to create achievement? While it's true that some of these categories overlap, it is safe to say that a significant number of students in every classroom are in dire need of someone capable of making the educational world safe, which is to say, someone who "gets it."

In the late 1980s I received a wedding invitation from a young woman I had believed would never live long enough to have a wedding day. I met her when she was sixteen and came to me for therapy; she was a gifted athlete who was nevertheless a stranger to almost no street drug, and who *existed* on her rage. I never thought of her as a suicide; I simply expected her to drive a hundred miles an hour into a bridge abutment just because the existence of that abutment pissed her off. The wedding invitation brought a smile. Inside, scribbled in her own hand, was a note saying I was to be one of two special guests;

I had saved her life as a teenager. *Luck* had saved her life as a teenager, but I would proudly sit in the row reserved for family.

I was the second-tier special guest, however. The top-drawer, first-class, bull-goose special guest was her seventh-grade teacher, whom she hadn't seen since seventh grade. When I watched Jeannie, in her wedding gown, sprint full speed across the grass at the public park doubling as a wedding chapel that day, I remembered: the reason Jeannie thought I saved her life was that her life had been saved years earlier by Miss Bergen, a teacher who had listened to Jeannie's account of her world and not judged or diminished it in any way; nor had she denied Jeannie's feelings by openly doubting her account of what led to them. In our early sessions before Jeannie had built a trust in me, when she would propose an unsolvable problem, my best therapy was simply to say, "What would Miss Bergen say about that?" Just remembering her calmed Jeannie down some, and often she would come up with wise words à la Miss Bergen.

I worked full time as a child and family therapist for nearly fifteen years and still do part-time pro bono work, and I have yet to engage a junior high or high school student who didn't have a teacher somewhere who stood up for them, who listened and didn't judge. For those kids with the most dysfunctional parents, I often hang my chances for success on the strength of a student's relationship with that teacher. When I work with a student who is having trouble in school and ask in which class they are having the greatest success, it's never what they're best at; it's which teacher they like, which teacher shows them the respect of being a witness to their lives.

In days when our educational culture is so directed at quantitative rather than qualitative evaluation, when expression has taken a back seat to rote memory, we are in dire need of teachers who can transcend the trend and focus on relationship. There is no tougher job than that of teacher. You are asked to do at school what should be done in the home, at the same time you are required to demand academic proficiency. I believe when a teacher allows the expression of the hard times in a student's life, he or she has a much greater chance of helping them attain that academic proficiency. It's just a hell of a lot easier to learn when you feel safe.

—*Chris Crutcher*

Craft Notes

Anyone can write; all it takes is time.

—KURT VONNEGUT, JR.

*W*hen I was on the outside of writing, reading and loving it, but rarely doing it, authors were magicians. Shazaam! Writing appears. When I first began writing with my students, I read everything I could find about process, trying to figure out how writing came to be. Authors who wrote about their work gave me ideas for working through my own issues in writing and they gave me hope. The writing process is indeed a little magical—bursts of insight, ideas that appear when I'm not looking, a story that brings my friend to tears. But the magic comes contained within hours of craft. The craft is what I wanted revealed.

I have collected a few notes on my craft, particularly on the writing of the stories in this collection. I've learned that the writing process varies with each piece. Some pieces came together fairly easily, which made me nervous. Others came to be over months of time and countless revisions and rereadings. As Ralph Fletcher said, writers need choice, time, and response. I've needed all three to help my writing grow.

This section is broken into parts that correspond to the traditional process we've known as writing teachers for years. You'll see the kinds of activities that have helped me find a topic, how I've worked through a draft, how I've learned to reread a text under development, the revisions that improved a piece, and the process I use to polish a draft. These are not distinct categories: I find new topics in the midst of a draft I'm working on; I begin revising a story and it becomes a poem; I begin polishing an essay only to stumble upon a needed revision. I wish it were all cleaner than that, but it never is.

I hope that my journeys in writing might help you find a path to your own. We're all writers; it just takes time—and faith that the process we teach will work for us as well.

prewriting
> using quick writes to find stories
> changing topics
> watching my world

drafting
> the first try
> using narrative scenes to develop structure
> studying a mentor author to learn about voice
> finding the right voice for the piece
> when a line sends my piece in a new direction
> staying true to the story

rereading
> answering a reader's questions
> pondering different angles for a story
> teachers' writing group

revision
> adding detail
> compression
> the use of metaphor
> working through endings

polishing
> catching clichés
> an adverb hunt
> reading out loud
> proofreading for word proximity

letting go

Prewriting

USING QUICK WRITES TO FIND STORIES

Prewriting for "David" *(page 22)*

The story of this lost ten-year-old I taught two decades ago came to me during a quick write. With my students I begin writing workshop almost every day with a piece of poetry, an interesting photograph, or just a suggestion like "zoom in on one moment from last night and show that scene." We write for four to five minutes and that's it. We're mining our world for story.

On this day the prompt was to focus in like a camera on one memory and write. I chose David and as usual, I started with description. We wrote on two more quick writes that day, but I stayed with David's story. In fifteen minutes I had sketched out the problem—his alcoholism—and knew I had more to say. These short bursts of writing work well for me and my students. I know quick writes are practice, and with such a small amount of time to work I don't feel the pressure to come up with something big and important.

A few students shared their writing that day. I read mine. Corey, who sat near the front, was instantly enthusiastic. He wanted to know more about David. He wanted the whole story. Enthusiasm is contagious. I went home and wrote all evening.

CHANGING TOPICS

Prewriting for "do the math" *(page 84)*

I opened up the paper and saw "lazy" in bold letters at the center of a column in our local paper about one of my new teachers. I felt like a cartoon character: red-faced and steaming. During the week before I had been struggling to write an argument model for my class on a drug raid at a high school, but my heart wasn't in the issue or the genre. Suddenly it was. I scribbled notes—no orderly outline here, just a page of numbers and exclamations and then a rambling draft in my journal about all the columnist didn't understand. I wrote the piece many times, drafting through anger and profanity and ranting, until I found a way to level my tone. I was reluctant to change topics in the middle of our unit, but I watched how my process changed once I had a topic I cared about. The piece worked on me all day long: writing in my head as I drove to school; casting aside leads while I stood in the lunch line; weighing arguments while watching field hockey after school. A passionate connection to my topic sustained me through many drafts until I was satisfied with the piece.

It reminded me once again of the power of topics that matter. Ho-hum writing just isn't very stimulating. Last year my son had to write an argument for teaching *The Catcher in Rye* in tenth-grade English. He could take either side, which I suppose was his topic choice, but it was a thinly disguised "did you read the book?" kind of exercise and he knew it. The only thing he felt passionately about was his hatred for all things English. He followed the template; he wrote the paper; he collected his B and counted the days until the end of the term. I don't think we have enough time to waste it choosing topics for our students.

WATCHING MY WORLD

Prewriting "Lucas" *(page 36)*

The teaching life is filled with moments that live on in my thinking for years. The rushed conversation in the hall that reveals something important; the way early morning light settles on my students all engaged in writing; the student who stays up all night crafting an experience that has formed her, then arrives breathless to tell me all about it. I watch my world and take notes, sometimes in my head, sometimes in my journal. Writers are observers. When I read Lucy Calkins' *The Art of Teaching Writing* years ago, I was struck by this quote: "I write to hold what I find in my life in my hands and to declare it a treasure. I'm not very good at this. When I sit down at my desk, I'm like my students. 'Nothing happens in my life,' I say. I feel empty-handed. I want to get up and rush around, looking for something Big and Significant to put on the page. And yet, as a writer I have come to know that significance cannot be found, it must be grown." So I plant seeds in my journal and wait for them to sprout.

I have a picture of Lucas in a class book in my basement. I ran across it last summer when I was trying to find the floor of the storage room. There he was, still looking fragile—almost broken. And I remembered how hard he was working to adjust to changing schools, homes, neighborhoods, climates. That evening I wrote "Lucas" in my journal. I didn't have time to write about him, but I wanted to remind myself of that story. I looked for signs of Lucas in students I met in elementary schools through my literacy coaching work that fall. I recognized reluctance and the broken stillness that some students carry. I watched students who hang back from the others, who hug the wall at recess. They were all Lucas. Once I started noticing, the details came back with such clarity that I had to write.

Drafting

Drafting "score" *(page 105)*

L et it all in. Trust the gush. Write your way through the piece. I've heard it said in many ways and have seen the posters in writing classrooms: discovery draft, rough draft, initial draft—all implying a beginning, not a polished piece. I know that language, but when I wrote the first draft about our faculty Powder Puff football game, it was just awful. I haven't seen a "really crappy draft" poster yet, but it happens. How do you help a writer through the despair of words that fall far short of intention? Sometimes you can't. Abandoned stories fill my journals.

But if the writer cares about the piece, here's what I suggest. Don Graves asks, "What is your wish for this piece? Can you find one line in the piece that shows what this story is most about?" Notice how both focus on what might be working. When I'm finished with the first burst of story, sometimes I have forgotten why I started writing it in the first place. As I reread, I delete the lines that take me away from what I hope the piece will become. In class I've asked, "What is one thing this piece is really about?" and I've shown my students the revisions I've made after asking myself that question.

First drafts are the initial murky mucking about in the swamp, at least in my writing world. How we nudge our writers to next steps matters.

Drafting "our last day of school" *(page 39)*

W riters have decisions to make. One of the key ones for me is which scenes I'll use to show what I'm trying to tell. In this piece I had many to choose from; my work with this girl had left a vivid imprint. I wrote several that I didn't include. I wrote a scene of Darlene on the playground that showed how well she played with much younger kids, and how ill-fitted she was with her peers. I often had Darlene's help after school in my room, and I wrote a scene of just the two of us at the school as darkness came. I wrote another of the parent conference. I collected a series of snapshots about this child, and then considered Don's question again, "What is this piece most about?" in making my selections. I decided on scenes that would focus on stealing because those helped me tell the larger story.

I show my students how narrative scenes often anchor writing, even in unlikely genres. I use editorials and articles from *The New York Times* as well as novels, biography, and news articles in class. We look at how a scene can hook a reader, show a glimpse of another part of the world, present a problem, or help us connect in a simple way to a much more complex issue. We practice writing scenes: one moment from Thanksgiving weekend; the conversation at breakfast this morning; the story of the four minutes between classes; a moment you remember from recess in elementary school.

Scenes give a story structure like a life raft in a rolling ocean. You can write your way from one scene to the next and find a way to get to the end of that first draft. For a student who needs a plan to get started, I listen to what the student wants to tell. I take notes. Then we look at the possible scenes that can show the story. The writer often deviates from the plan, but it provides something to hold on to and a way to get started.

STUDYING A MENTOR AUTHOR TO LEARN ABOUT VOICE

Drafting "introduction: water and dawn and bait"
(page 1)

I've read *Bird by Bird* and *Traveling Mercies* by Anne Lamott at least three times each and every novel she's written once. I also inhale the writing of Leonard Pitts, Jr., and Mitch Albom. I don't just read; I study. I consider phrasing and sentence structure and style. Those qualities create voice. I pay attention to their writing because their voices are so approachable. I encourage my students to choose an author to study throughout the semester. When you become familiar with one author's work you'll begin to attend to the idiosyncrasies of that writer and then learn to attend to your own.

One of the qualities of voice is the author's distance from the topic and from the reader. In this book I wanted to establish a conversation, and I tuned my voice carefully in the introduction to be invitational and close. "Silence is downright marvelous"; "You'll be blamed for not keeping that fish on your line; it's just the way it is"; "It's why teachers are such pack rats, by the way." This is how I talk with my students and my friends. I end the piece by saying, "I'd like to share a few secrets I've learned," which implies a whispered confession for your ears alone and invites you to turn the page and keep reading. I've felt Anne's work do that to me many times: she draws me close and I feel like she is writing for me alone.

FINDING THE RIGHT VOICE FOR THE PIECE

Drafting "honors: a teacher's reeducation" *(page 68)*

I found the beginning of this piece in an entry in my writing notebook that I'd scribbled one day after an administrator told me he could judge the worth of a teacher by the level of students they taught. "Anyone can teach AP and honors kids," he had said. I disagreed. Teaching honors kids pushed me, but in a different way than other students had. I began with a voice in conversation, speaking directly to the administrator. But then I found I was talking to myself, looking at my own developing understanding of working with these students. When I began detailing the individual traits of my students, I was writing for them. In each case I can find places where I've tailored my words for the audience I'm imagining. That's what I have to help my students see in their work.

I admit it's tricky. I used to coach my students to find their own unique voice or to imitate speech, neither of which worked very well. We all have many voices; the trick is to match the right voice to the particular focus of the piece. I show this in our letter-writing unit. My students write three letters: one personal, one professional, and one persuasive. They choose the audience and subject of each, but their goal is to be aware of how they use voice differently depending on the audience. Anna chose a letter to her mother, a letter in support of a friend's admission to Williams College, and a letter to our community paper. In each case you could feel Anna, but the tone, style, and language of the letters differed considerably. Making her attend to those differences helps her develop an understanding of how she can craft her voice for the purpose of the piece.

WHEN A LINE SENDS MY PIECE IN A NEW DIRECTION

Drafting "the traffic cop" *(page 88)*

"I am learning nothing in this class," appeared in the middle of my first rambling draft about my former student. That one line came to me and I could see Ken standing at the door of my room in his leather jacket, rocking from one foot to the other, his blue eyes glaring. I winced as I recalled it, but I could feel my anger and hurt as I wrote. I started drafting faster, focused in a new way.

The first time I reread my essay, I cut everything before that sentence. I had been trying to describe him, fumbling about for the right words, but when he walked in my room and spit that out, I saw him.

I can plan all morning and then sit to write a piece and find directions I hadn't thought of. The act of writing takes me back and uncovers moments I had forgotten, but I often have to write through uncertainty to get there. I need more writing, less planning, to find a story.

Drafting "Penny" *(page 17)*

It was my sixth birthday. I peed on the floor during the pledge of allegiance. I had a mean teacher that I remember well. Our family was in the midst of my father's battle with alcoholism. Those are the facts. Although I have strong imprints of particular details from that morning—my teacher's glasses, walking back to my desk, the scuffle after it happened—I couldn't remember the name of the student who shouted for my teacher's attention. I wasn't sure which dress my mom had sewn for me, or if on that particular night she had stayed up all night sewing. I had many memories of outfits she had made for me and the love she had put into each one. In crafting this story I used both what I distinctly remembered and what I invented to make the experience live for a reader. As William Zinsser says, "Memoir is the art of inventing the truth." What matters is that the author stays true to the story; the details are secondary. My story from that day is true, particularly my perspective as a child in that classroom.

When I teach memoir in class I use anchor texts like "Eleven" from *Woman Hollering Creek*, by Sandra Cisneros. I have my students consider which details might have been invented to show the truth of the story. I might use a paragraph from a piece I'm writing and show where I feel I need to add detail in order to put the reader into the scene with me. If I can't recall it, I make it up, but I'm careful to have the detail be insignificant and not alter the truth of the story. It's a tool all writers can access: use the look and feel of today's snowfall to tell about a moment from last winter.

Rereading

Rereading "grace" *(page 27)*

This piece started with rolling my Mini Cooper into a Jeep outside of our school about a month after I bought it. In my journal ranting I could picture my husband's exasperation, his saying, "You're the absentminded professor!" But I also remembered I was thinking about a student's pregnancy at the time, and I started listing all of the times thinking about one thing had distracted me from what I was doing. The list was mighty long. Clearly, there was a pattern.

When I reread the entry and the list, the moment on that playground jumped out. I drafted that scene. I shared it with a writing friend who said, "So what? Why did breaking your nose on the playground matter?" I couldn't answer my friend that day, but I kept turning it over in my head and found the theme for the piece. Sometimes I sit alone with my writing and ask my own questions. It works, but it isn't nearly as revealing as the questions I'm asked in writing group.

Rereading "Kleenex and marriage and learning to teach" *(page 76)*

As I explained in this story, I started taking notes as my husband was talking that morning, sure that I was learning something about responding to writers. But there's a big difference between listing and note-taking and crafting an essay. Moving from one to the other required me to consider ways I could approach the story.

My first draft included my frustrations with writing that morning. In my second draft I started with him reading, but after the confrontation I struggled with the rest of the story. Should I take the reader into my classroom or keep us on the couch? And once in the classroom, which writers should I show?

Wrestling with writing decisions helps me coach a student who says, "I don't know what to write." None of us do. The possibilities are endless. Go with one and see what happens.

TEACHERS' WRITING GROUP

Rereading "Katelyn" *(page 58)*

We all want professional development that matters. We hate wasting time. A few colleagues and I have found the answer. We meet when we can and we share our writing. It is always an energizer; no pressure, just friends to nudge you along and celebrate what you are able to do, then offer ideas and perspectives that you haven't thought of. Because we struggle inside the process, we are better writing teachers.

In the case of an early draft of "Katelyn," I needed coaching. I had four stories fighting for space and I kept trying to pack them all into one essay anyway. There was Katelyn's writing piece of many parts, my struggle to coach her in different kinds of conferences, the drag race on prom night, the Powder Puff football game. My piece was like that pair of jeans fresh out of the dryer; I couldn't stretch it any farther and it was mighty uncomfortable. My writing group buddies first told me all the lines they liked, all the images that stayed with them, all the reasons I should keep working on the story. Boy, does that stuff matter. Next they told me where they had to reread because they were confused and where the focus changed.

I left that afternoon smiling.

I had problems, but I had a plan. Not only for "Katelyn," but for the next writer who will come to me with the same problem. Now I can say, "This is what I tried . . ." and our writer-to-writer conference will enrich us both.

Revision

ADDING DETAIL

Revision in "stopping at a lunchroom table" *(page 31)*

In draft one I wrote dialogue only. It was a conversation that carried the meaning in this story, and I tried to remember every word. On the first rereading I could feel the absence of image. It was like eavesdropping on a phone call: I only had part of the story. I put myself back in the cafeteria and turned off the sound in my head. I saw Sean dipping his head into his polar fleece jacket; I saw the smiling lunch ladies, the chocolate donuts wrapped in cellophane. We see more than we realize.

I often suggest a focus for the rereading of a draft and model it for my students. I will share just a paragraph of a piece I'm working on and focus on sensory detail. Is there a sound I could add? In "second chance" the scrape of the metal chair leg against the linoleum floor gave me the transition I was looking for in that piece. Is there a smell that will help the reader connect? Smell moves us. I cleaned up cat urine yesterday—tell me you didn't wince when you read that line. Smell is powerful: stop by my house on a Saturday morning in time for cinnamon scones; I'll convince you.

COMPRESSION

Revision of "confessions" *(page 81)*

This writing piece began in three parts. There was a scene in my office, a scene at my house, and a scene in the hall at school. I had the student perspective, then the teacher's, then another student's. My writing group was confused by the number of characters I had in the piece, as well as the number of locations. Too much was going on at once; especially considering my message was pretty simple. They suggested I try two scenes instead of three. Deleting one section improved momentum and minimized confusion. It was a smart editing move, but it was painful. Cutting words often is. Writers get married to structure, to story, to a few lines that sing. We have to be gentle with revision suggestions.

I've started asking a Don Graves revision question: Can you find a sentence or scene that your story is *least* about? Instead of asking a student to find the center of a piece, I'm asking them to find what doesn't serve to focus the reader on that center. The student finds the place where compression improves the focus of the text. We share these findings in class.

THE USE OF METAPHOR

Revision for "my first steelie" *(page 11)*

I didn't see Jerry as a fish I was trying to catch until many drafts into the piece. Often as I near the end of the work on a piece, I reread the first draft to see if there's anything essential that I've cut that I shouldn't have. In my notebook I had written quite a bit about fishing with my dad and the morning when I caught my first steelhead. These few sentences got me thinking:

> I was determined not to lose this fish no matter how it fought me. Reel in. Let run. Reel again steady and wait as the line bobbed and weaved with the fight of a fish in flight. Man against fish—a delightful battle.

Suddenly I just knew: Jerry and I were in a battle. The metaphor appeared. What if Jerry became the steelie I was trying to land? My energy soared at the possibility. I began threading references to the metaphor throughout the piece.

My journey with this extended metaphor has helped me coach student writers in using this strategy. I have my students find the fishing references in the piece as they read. We underline with colored pencils and share what we've found. I hope the work might inspire a few to try it. Some have. Most have not. I recognize this is part of the process. I knew how extended metaphors were woven into writing for years, but I never tried it. Just like catching that first steelhead, in my case it took a lot of time on the water before I nailed one.

I would never assign "write an extended metaphor" to anyone. Writing should always be about the writer's vision for the piece first, and the possibilities for telling the story arise as the text does.

WORKING THROUGH ENDINGS

Revision of "Josh" *(page 33)*

This piece is still not finished as I write today. I've written at least six different endings so far. The story is pretty straightforward and I breezed through the first page with a deep sense of what I wanted to show. But then I ended with how hard it is to be a teacher with parents asking us to do these impossible things. I felt like I should add a little violin music to my whine. Cut. What a satisfying little keystroke that is!

Should I end by telling you that Josh steered clear of me after that? He wouldn't meet my eyes in class; he stopped laughing at my jokes. It's true. But it sounds so depressing.

Should I tell you how I would handle it today with all of my experience? I tried that, too. I thought I wrote something pretty snappy, but when Eben, one of my writing group buddies, and I met, he said, "What happened to the kid? You just dropped him." Curses. And then he continued, "Why did you put this Garrison Keillor quote at the top if all of your effort really was wasted?" Thanks, Eben.

I ask myself over and over again, "What am I trying to say?" So that's what I write: an answer to that question. I talk to my notebook; I talk to my fellow teachers.

I had this kid once named Josh. And if I could go back . . .

I'll find that ending.

Polishing

Polishing is a last step. It would be hard to say exactly when a piece moves from revision to polishing. I feel a shift in my reading of the piece, from trying to hear the story and make big decisions about what to include, to a microscopic focus on every word. However, there are times when I think I'm cruising through polishing a last read and I stumble on an entire scene that suddenly doesn't belong. It forces me to consider the whole of the piece again, and if I cut the scene, I have to rethink the scene that follows. I go backward in my process. Pretty soon I'm mucking about in a draft again looking for a path. I wish I could tell you it is simpler than that, but it hasn't been. Sometimes one step folds back onto another and you start again.

Catching Clichés

Polishing "multigenre marriage" *(page 99)*

Within a few days of Pat's visit to my classroom I wrote a draft of that moment. In the first paragraph I had this line:

It was just like Dickens: you know, the best and worst of times.

It was in reference to the fact that it was a great day because the holiday vacation would follow and it was also my anniversary, but it was also horrible to try to contain my students when they just wanted to party. The line nagged at me. I left it in draft after draft, even when I knew it was a cliché. Part of polishing, though, is paying attention to the things that nag you.

I spotted my writing pal Ed reading my piece while on lunch duty and said, "What about the Dickens thing?"

He shook his head. "I thought about that, but I didn't know if I should say anything. It's a cliché; it should go." Aaaaargh. Caught again, then saved by a thirty-second writing conference. I find clichés in my writing all the time. They are weak. Always. In my classroom we'll spend ten minutes rereading a draft for just that one thing. Then we slice and dice 'em.

AN ADVERB HUNT

Polishing "one large to go, extra cheese" *(page 94)*

Here's what I know about adverbs. They're clutter. Useless. Most of the time they don't add to an image, they club the reader over the head. I hunt for them as I revise and eliminate almost all of them. Initially the verbs look kind of forlorn left alone in a sentence, but once the adverbs are gone, I don't miss them. And I pay more attention to those verbs: the engine of the sentence.

Here are two I found in a draft of "one large to go, extra cheese."

She paused deliberately.
I smiled warmly.

Overkill. You can hear it. They were easy to toss. It is writing that is trying too hard.

READING OUT LOUD

Polishing "Emily" *(page 64)*

Okay, this is a secret. It was the day before my first book signing. I was holding my book in my lap, admiring it once again I must admit, when the phone rang. Don called to ask which pieces I would be reading. I said I didn't know. He said, "Which ones sound the best out loud?" My cheeks flushed and I panicked. I had no idea; I'd never read any of them out loud. I know writers say they do this, but I didn't. I hung up the phone and started reading "of frog legs, crickets, and Superman's cape" from *Public Teaching: One Kid at a Time* in a room in the basement with the door shut. Quietly.

I reached for a pencil.

I had changes to make. I saw my stories differently as I spoke the words out loud. It is truly a different way to hear a text. It was too late to make changes at that point, but I've made reading aloud a regular part of my process since. I read to my husband, my daughter, my son, and my dog. The cats ignore me.

I read "Emily" to a small gathering of teachers when I first began drafting the piece. When I read this line, "Emily glanced out the window as grief made a quick journey from her eyes to the lines around her mouth," Lucie let out a little "Oh." I knew that line had power. I went home and read it out loud again. Then I got back to writing.

PROOFREADING FOR WORD PROXIMITY

Polishing "beginning" *(page 5)*

In the panic of my first day of teaching I prayed many times. *Lord, help me* was a thumping little background beat to my day. I found myself repeating that phrase as I drafted the story. When rereading I thought my little prayers were kind of clever: you can spout all you want to about separation of church and state, but give me a new teacher and believe me, prayer returns to the classroom. Repetition in writing is annoying to a reader, though. I started deleting the phrase and replacing it with *yikes, oh no,* and other variations on my internal talk.

In the first paragraph of "beginning" I had written that my day "crawled along." In the next scene I found "the minute hand crawled toward lunch." It had to go; the phrases were too close together. Words and images lose their power when repeated in close proximity. Sometimes those words survive through many drafts because I'm focused elsewhere, but when I put time into polishing I usually hear them.

Letting Go

When I first read these words in *Life of Pi* by Yann Martel, I was working on the ending for this book. "It's important in life to conclude things properly. Only then can you let go. Otherwise you are left with words you should have said but never did, and your heart is heavy with remorse." I felt the pressure to conclude "properly" with my writing, but I wasn't sure how to. I sweated for weeks.

Don Murray told me, "Art is never finished, only abandoned." I tried to abandon mine. I took the manuscript to work with me so it could sit on my desk and remind me it was still there. I carried it from one room in my house to another. I had it open on my lap in the car when I drove around town. I reread it at intersections, looking for last-minute changes, but you should definitely not tell my husband about that. And then I had to slide it across the counter at my local post office and quit reaching for it.

There's a time when the writer is finished, even if the writing still has flaws. The story has been told; the energy for revision is gone. Even if there are words left to be said that I just can't find. It's time to move on to new thinking and new writing. My stories now travel out into the world, wrinkles and all. I will no doubt wish I could still make changes, but it's time to let go. That's just another part of the writing process.

acknowledgments

Writing takes time. Life takes time.
There's your problem. Can they happen together?
They can.

—KIM STAFFORD

Once upon a time in an old church in downtown Portland, Oregon, Pat and I were joined in marriage on a snowy evening. He's been beside me through twenty years of students and stories and the exhaustion of trying to do this work well. He's listened patiently as I've worked through what to include in this book, and agreed to take-out food because none of the revisions went well again. Pat's my biggest fan, my closest friend. He is always at the end it seems, after our own kids, teaching, writing, and even the dog and cats, I'm afraid. Pat's wise and kind. He's generous and loyal. I couldn't have written this without him.

My son, Cam, and my daughter, Hannah, continue to teach me about parenting and life. They sat in the front row at my first book signing. They laugh when I need it, cook marvelous soups, and do the laundry. Really. They are passionate and feisty and loving. Every day is richer because of them.

I've learned well over the last four years that writing won't grow without encouragement and careful listening. When *Public Teaching: One Kid at a Time* (2003) was published I waited anxiously for a response from friends, family, and colleagues. Theresa Kennett, Tom Jolliff, Renee Harrah, and Karen Franke were enthusiastic and so darn nice about my work. They gave me the energy to keep writing. This book was born of their encouragement.

Tom Romano saved this manuscript when it was headed for the dumpstah (as they say here in the North Country.) Tom wrote my introduction and saw more in what I was writing than I did. He was patient as I reorganized and emailed and agonized. He's not only tolerant, he's the ultimate teacher.

Don Graves continues to anchor the most important professional collaboration of my life. His vision of writing classrooms has shaped my teaching at every grade level. His funny sayings litter my journal entries and his passion for helping others inspires me. But mostly it is our writing conferences that fuel my work. He reads and shares and listens and nods. Then he helps me see differently. Meanwhile Betty feeds us and gives me his time. Thank you, Betty.

I am grateful to Chris Crutcher for agreeing to write the afterword for this book. I have admired his writing for years, particularly his regular column in *Voices from the Middle*. Chris always makes me want to try harder, understand more, and listen harder to the students that I teach.

I also must acknowledge the writing of Anne Lamott. Both *Bird by Bird* and *Traveling Mercies* have illuminated the writing process and have helped me teach writing to teenagers. Anne's faith stories inspire and teach me and make me want to get back to writing my own.

Lois Bridges is to editing what Johnny Depp is to pirates: it doesn't get any better than this. Lois is quick and funny and so nice. I think she ought to write a book filled with the right things to say to the wrong writing pieces. She manages to salvage even my most troubled stories with her wisdom and her faith. The rest of the crew at Heinemann, especially Lesa Scott, Maura Sullivan, Leigh Peake, Lisa Fowler, Kevin Carlson, Lynne Costa, Jenny Jensen Greenleaf, Jen Noon, and Alison Maloney are the smart professionals I aspire to be.

Years ago I had Ken Fowler in my eighth-grade language arts class at Kennett Junior High School in Conway. I assigned a persuasive essay and he wrote "Why all teachers should be put in jail for the psychological trauma they inflict on helpless students." The piece was so well written I had him read it to each of my five classes. Ken was a talent, but a troubled one. When I moved to the high school years later, he was in my freshman class as a repeater. We had a rough go of it, and it broke my heart. I was pleased when he completed his GED and went to work at Waldenbooks in North Conway. I stop by and see him every once in awhile, thrilled he is content. When I started writing this book I wanted to tell the stories of students who drop out of school, because there are too many. I designed my "narrative in two voices" because I wanted a student to tell his side of the story. That student was Ken. I was pretty relentless in my nagging, and he gave in and wrote the piece. I did a little dance when I held it in my hands. I applaud his courage in letting us all hear what high school means for some kids. We need to listen.

My former students live in my heart. In the writing of this book I want to thank in particular Nick Gunn, Emily Clancy, Matt Wright, Sean McGee, and Heather Vendola.

At my small school in New Hampshire I have spent a lot of time talking about teaching with two passionate and committed educators who are the most inspiring leaders I've ever known. Jack Loynd and Kevin Richard work hard, love kids, and make decisions with the greatest integrity. I know they have made a lasting imprint on my teaching. My writing colleagues: Ed Fayle, Ryan Mahan, Joe Fernald, Eben Plese, Carrie Costello, and Reed Van Rossum have laughed at all the right places and always prodded me to do more. God, I love them for that.

My seniors in Essay Writing at Kennett High School in Conway during the fall of 2003 and the fall of 2004 read many of these pieces as I struggled to teach writing by showing them my process. Their laughter and suggestions helped me continue to craft my writing. Their willingness to take risks in their own writing made me continue to love teaching. Thank you, Sean Ashe, Marc Bamberger, Sabrina Basu, Shawn Bergeron, Melissa Bornheim, Krista Chadwick,

Christina Coleman, Jon Desillier, Carrie Doe, Alex Else, Todd Frechette, Matt Gagnon, Krystal Gilmore, Ryann Gordon, Nicole Gunn, Corey Gray, Ben Hacket, Pat Haine, Molly Hamilton, Alex Hamlin, Tyler Haynes, Kyle Hickey, Julie Hirshan, Elliott Irvin, Liz Kantack, John Karmozyn, Tanner Kennett, MacKenzie Maher-Colville, Kathleen Maynard, Emma McCleavey-Weedern, Sarah Morrison, Chris Murphy, Kyle Nason, Alex Norden, Heidi Noriega, Gus Owen, Taylor Peer, Scott Pelletier, Katelyn Quint, Sierra Roberts, Brian Roy, Tom Santasanio, Leanne Smith, Tim Smith, Jay Spencer, Chet Trundy, Ben Wagner, Christine Willenbrock, Sarah Wood, and Billy Worcester. I still miss you guys each morning. Trust me, if all classes were like this, we'd never have a teaching shortage.